# How To Have Peace in Difficult Times

# How to Have Peace in Difficult Times

*Staying calm*
*no matter what's going*
*on around you*

## David L. Johnston

PUBLISHING & MARKETING
Oviedo, FL

# Table of Contents

# Introduction

The cross is God's great plus sign. Through its power, God continually adds good things to our hearts and minds. He is the best friend we will ever have. In the pages that follow, you will discover how the cross of Christ is the greatest source of peace for your heart. It has been said that if peace is not inside you, there is no use looking for it anywhere else. Peace must become part of our heart's operating system. The heart runs the operating system and the mind runs the software, and it is vital that they work together. As a muscle, the heart keeps blood flowing throughout our bodies, while the brain is the central control system for the heart and other bodily functions. When our physical heart or brain lacks peace, *our entire body* can be negatively affected.

Peace is a realm that exists in your heart and your mind, one in which chaos is not allowed to enter. Chaos shows itself in a variety of forms: anger, depression, panic, worry, or mistrust. Peace, on the other hand, is the absence of these and any other negative feelings and emotions. So what's the big deal?

When a person's mind and heart are led by real peace, they can make wise decisions; but anger, anxiety, bitterness, or strife disrupts that peace. When that happens, that person's thinking ability, powers of observation, and decision-making skills can all be corrupted. Since a person's wisdom can be rendered null and void without real peace guiding the way, it is vital that God's peace be the core condition of your soul. That's how desperately we need it in its proper place.

In the chapters that follow, we will discover what genuine peace is, how it transforms our lives, and how we can maintain that peace—with God, ourselves, and others. Each chapter details important aspects of peace and supports its points with the Word of God.

In chapter one, we will discover God's perspective on peace. God actually weeps over the *absence* of peace. The good news is that peace was accomplished for us by the work of Christ on the cross and in the empty tomb. That peace is maintained in us by the good works God enables us to do after we have been reconciled to Him, so that His peace affects every aspects of our lives—now and in the future. In fact, we are God's ambassadors of peace to the world. Peace should encompass our entire lives. It is the hallmark of our relationship with God.

In chapters two and three, we will examine God's path for living in genuine peace. God does not leave us in the dark about achieving peace in our lives. His Word perfectly explains how we can have peace with Him, peace with others, and internal peace within ourselves. We will also look at the differences between God's genuine peace and the false peace the world offers, and understand why we must not be casual about peace in our lives, but actively pursue it because peace begets peace and leads us to triumph. We will also take a brief look at the important role that prayer and the Holy Spirit play in maintaining our peace.

In chapter four, we will focus on the *power* of God's peace. One important way that God's peace is different from the world's peace is that it comes with real power. We will look at seven ways that peace gives us power when we are controlled by God's Word and Spirit.

In the last chapter, we will discover how peaceful speech will bring joy into our hearts. All people seek true joy, but often are not sure how to find it. The secret lies in a peaceful heart that governs a peaceful tongue.

It is my hope that this book will help you know true peace. Since peace is central to our well-being and all our relationships, we can be thankful that God has shown us His path to peace. God has not left us wandering in the dark. We can know true peace through our Lord Jesus Christ.

# Chapter 1

# The Greatest Symbol of Peace

*"And the peace of God, which passeth all understanding, shall keep your hearts and minds through Christ Jesus."*
(Philippians 4:7)

P hilippians 4:7 is a key verse to which we will return often. According to the Bible, the source of all peace is Christ's work on the cross and His resurrection from the grave. This core of the gospel provides us with what Paul calls "the peace that passeth understanding." The word *understanding* in this context refers to comprehending the relationship between cause and effect: A causes B which causes C. According to Paul, this exchange between us and Jesus gives us a peace that is beyond our comprehension. We may not be able to grasp the cause-and-effect relationship between the cross and peace, but it is still true. Just because this peace is beyond our human understanding does not make it any less of a reality; instead, it fundamentally changes our hearts and minds.

# 1. God Weeps over the Lack of Peace

Before we discover how God achieved this peace for us, we must understand how important peace is to God. God is not a cold and impersonal Being. He cares deeply for His creation, especially people. In the Bible, God yearns for His people. He hurts when they hurt. He grieves over their fallen condition. He pours Himself out to rescue them. As every event in our history plays out, God is never a disinterested bystander. He's in the thick of things all the time, and the absence of peace greatly troubles Him. He weeps over the lack of peace. Whenever people needed Him and cried out to Him, He met them in their trouble. That's who He is.

When the Israelites were weeping over the destruction of their temple, this was God's direction to them:

> *"Then he said unto them, Go your way, eat the fat, and drink the sweet, and send portions unto them for whom nothing is prepared: for this day is holy unto our Lord: neither be ye sorry; for **the joy of the Lord** is your strength."* (Nehemiah 8:10)

He pointed His people to Himself as the Source of their joy. This remains the same today: The joy of the Lord gives us strength. The joy that the Lord has over our life strengthens us to follow His commands and stay in His peace—no matter what. He promises to strengthen us and bring sweet joy into each of our lives. In times of sorrow, we have access to God's joy and can find our strength and peace in Him.

**God is never a disinterested bystander.**

Additionally, sometimes God Himself weeps over the state of the world. Luke provides a moving example of this from the life of Jesus. When Jesus first came to Jerusalem, He mourned over the city's rejection of His message of peace for mankind.

> *"And when he was come near, he beheld the city, and wept over it,*
>
> *Saying, if thou hadst known, even thou, at least in this thy day, the things which belong unto thy peace! but now they are hid from thine eyes."*        (Luke 19:41-42)

Jesus wept over them because they were rejecting their Messiah and the peace He could bring them. Because of this rejection, peace would flee from the city of Jerusalem. Jesus knew what was in store for them because of their poor choices and was pierced to the point of weeping. He knew they did not know how to have peace.

God has those same feelings for you. He desires your peace and well-being. When you live without peace, He is deeply grieved. Since Jesus is the Prince of Peace, He is especially aware of how important it is for His people to share His peace, and what a terrible thing it is for any of them to live without it.

## 2. Peace Is the Message of the Cross

> *"And suddenly there was with the angel a multitude of the heavenly host praising God, and saying,*
>
> *Glory to God in the highest, and on earth peace, good will toward men."*
>
>                                (Luke 2:13-14)

Peace was provided by Jesus on the cross of Calvary, but long before Calvary, peace was fundamental to Christ's mission. The angels' praises at Christ's birth was focused on peace for all mankind. God became man and came to earth to bring peace—personal peace to each and every soul. The angels foretold this mission and praised God for it.

> *"For he hath made him to be sin for us,*
> *who knew no sin; that we might be made*
> *the righteousness of God in him."*
> (2 Corinthians 5:21)

Peace is still central to Christ's mission today. It didn't stop at the manger. Jesus Christ was made sin for us. Can you imagine that? God was made into the very thing which He hated most. When Jesus went to the cross, He took upon Himself the sin of all time, so that we might have God's forgiveness. God has not only forgiven us, He has also given us peace through the blood of His cross.

## Jesus' sacrifice brought peace to mankind and the entire created order.

> *"And, **having made peace through the blood of his cross**, by him to reconcile all things unto himself; by him, I say, whether they be things in earth, or things in heaven."* (Colossians 1:20)

Think about it. Peace came through the blood of His cross. He came so you could have peace, and He died so you could have peace. We'll explore some of the reasons why this is so, but first, let's go back to Golgotha. Jesus was beaten by His own people, and then turned over to Roman soldiers, who scourged Him with whips, drove a crown of thorns onto His head, mocked Him, and abused Him even more. Then, they led Him up to the hill called Golgotha, and crucified God the Son. Something amazing happened on that cross that changed everything. On the cross (just as Jesus foretold in John 3:14-17), *Christ was made sin on our behalf.*

Through His sacrifice on the cross, Christ was able to reconcile all things unto Himself—break down all the barriers. The cross reconciles all things unto Christ—in heaven, on the earth, and under the earth. *All things.* That is what He did. That was the work of the cross. Jesus' sacrifice brought peace to mankind and the entire created order. This is the good news.

## Why Jesus Went to the Cross

In one passage, the prophet Isaiah tells us that Christ went to the cross for four important reasons.

> *"Surely he hath borne our griefs, and carried our sorrows: yet we did esteem him stricken, smitten of God, and afflicted.*
>
> *But he was wounded for our transgressions, he was bruised for our iniquities: the* ***chastisement of our peace was upon him;*** *and with his stripes we are healed."*
>
> (Isaiah 53:4-5)

These verses outline those reasons. Through His work on the cross, Jesus took care of the following:

1. Our transgressions
   *"He was wounded for our transgressions,"* that is, our sins.
2. Our iniquities
   *"He was bruised for our iniquities."*
3. Our peace
   And then, *"the chastisement of our peace was upon Him."*
4. Our healing
   *"And with His stripes we are healed."*

Verse 5 says: "The chastisement of our peace was upon Him." There, on the cross, Jesus, God the Son, made peace for us through the shedding of His blood, satisfying the Law of Moses, and destroying the barriers between us and God for all time.

> *"And almost all things are by the law purged with blood; and **without shedding of blood is no remission**."* (Hebrews 9:22)

Jesus took our punishment and gave us peace with God. Without this peace, there could be no hope of salvation, and no hope of peace in this world. He still does this today. We give Him our anxiety and trouble and He gives us His peace in exchange.

# 3. Peace Is the Message of the Empty Tomb

> *"He is not here: for **he is risen**, as he said. Come, see the place where the Lord lay."*
> (Matthew 28:6)

Christ's message of peace does not stop at the cross. It culminates in the resurrection. We know the story: After Jesus was crucified on Golgotha, the soldiers pierced His side with a spear. Blood and water poured out. They killed Jesus. They killed God, God the Son. Can you imagine that? It is recorded that even the soldiers were aware that Jesus was no ordinary criminal.

Then, they buried Him in a tomb, and rolled a big stone across it to seal him inside. A few days later, one of Jesus' followers went to see the tomb; when she arrived, she got the biggest shock of her life! An angel greeted her with the words: "He is not here. He is risen." *The tomb was empty.* Jesus was not there. His grave clothes were still over in a corner, but He was gone. Jesus had been raised from the dead just as He'd predicted. His faithful follower ran back and told everybody, "He's not there! He is risen!" So what does this have to do with peace?

> *"Then the same day at evening, being the first day of the week, when the doors were shut where the disciples were assembled for fear of the Jews, **came Jesus and stood in the midst, and saith unto them, Peace be unto you.**"* (John 20:19)

Mary Magdalene told the disciples that she had seen the Lord and that He had spoken to her. That very evening, the disciples locked themselves up in a room because of their great fear. Suddenly Jesus appeared and stood in their midst, and said to them, "Peace be unto you." This was His first message after the resurrection, a message of complete peace. John continues his account by saying:

> *"And when he had so said, he shewed unto them his hands and his side. Then were the disciples glad, when they saw the Lord.*
>
> *Then said Jesus to them again, **Peace be unto you**: as my Father hath sent me, even so send I you."*      (John 20:20-21)

Jesus confirmed to His disciples that He was indeed the risen Lord by showing them His hands and side. The disciples were relieved and encouraged (gladdened). Jesus repeated His message of peace and commanded them to bring that message to the world, but He did not stop there. Just a few verses later, we read:

> *"And after eight days again his disciples were within, and Thomas with them: then came Jesus, the doors being shut, and stood in the midst, and said, **Peace be unto you**."*
>                                                        (John 20:26)

After eight days again, the disciples were together in the upper room, and Thomas who had been absent the first time was now present. The risen Christ, who has such molecular control of the universe that He is able to walk through closed doors, stood with the disciples again. Christ declared the same message: "Peace be unto you." This message of peace was repeated three times after His resurrection. Like being born-again, peace is Christ's focal point to humanity. His peace is part and parcel to our salvation experience, the first fruit of our relationship with Him. And so He repeated it: "Peace be unto you."

# 4. His Peace Is Imparted and Conveyed to Us

> *"The LORD will give strength unto his*
> *people;* **the LORD will bless his people**
> **with peace.***"*          (Psalm 29:11)

Look carefully at this delightful psalm. The peace which Christ bought at the cross is for you today. The Lord continually gives strength to His people, and blesses His people with peace. This perfect peace is promised to you by the Lord.

> *"Peace I leave with you,* **my peace I give**
> **unto you**: *not as the world giveth, give I*
> *unto you. Let not your heart be troubled,*
> *neither let it be afraid."*          (John 14:27)

Jesus does not give as the world does. The peace of Christ is a gift from Him—freely given. It cancels out anxiety and fear. Jesus imparts His peace to us supernaturally. As mentioned before, His peace passes our understanding. It is a result of knowing Christ, and has nothing to do with our works. Many believers have struggled with this concept. This story illustrates the point:

A young man was eager to grow in His Christian life. He got a piece of paper and made a list of all the things he would do for God. He wrote down the things he would give up, the places he would go to minister, and the areas of ministry he would enter. He was excited. He took that list to the church and put it on the altar.

He thought he would feel joy, but instead he felt empty.

So he went home and started adding to his list. He wrote down more things he would do and wouldn't do. He took the longer list and put it on the altar, but still he felt nothing.

Finally, he went to a wise, old pastor, told him the situation, and asked for help. The pastor said, "Take a blank sheet of paper. Sign your name at the bottom. Put *that* on the altar." The young man did, and then peace came to his heart.[1]

Jesus actually just wants us—as we are. He does have plans for each of us, but more than anything, He simply wants us. He will transform us as we walk with Him. He will make changes in us too—wonderful changes, but His love is fixed upon us in such a way that He enjoys dwelling with us. It's hard to imagine that the Master of the Universe would actually feel that way about us, but He does. His gift of peace cannot be separated from knowing Him. It comes with the territory.

Once we know Jesus, our job is to abide in Him, allowing Him to work through us.

# 5. Peace Is Maintained by Allowing God to Work in Us

> *"The wicked, through the pride of his countenance, will not seek after God: **God is not in all his thoughts.***
>
> *His ways are always grievous; thy judgments are far above out of his sight: as*

---

1    R. B. Ouellette, *The Pulling down of Strongholds: Learning to Live in Freedom from Wrong Thinking* (Murfreesboro, TN: Sword of the Lord Publishers, 2009).

*for all his enemies, he puffeth at them."*
(Psalm 10:4-5)

In these verses, the psalmist provides a contrast for us, comparing the wicked to those who keep their minds on the Lord. There will always be those who do not accept God's gift of peace. The wicked do not seek after God. Instead they are led by their own pride and have no regard for God at all. Here's the same verse from the *New American Standard Bible*:

> *"The wicked, in his haughtiness, does not seek Him.* **There is no God** *in all his schemes."*      (Psalm 10:4 NASB)

God is not in all their thoughts. As a result, they live as laws unto themselves. Since God is not on the throne of their hearts, they're brazen in their lifestyle choices. However, when things go badly they have nothing to stand on. However this is not the way of life God wants for anyone. His alternative is so much better.

> *"**Thou wilt keep him in perfect peace**, whose mind is stayed on thee: because he trusteth in thee."*      (Isaiah 26:3)

In contrast, God maintains His perfect peace in those who trust in Him. Peace is promised to us, but it is maintained by keeping our thoughts on the Lord, a process God helps us with as we grow. Isaiah continues a few verses later:

> **"LORD, thou wilt ordain peace for us**: *for thou also hast wrought all our works in us."* (Isaiah 26:12)

God is doing something in us. He has ordained peace for us and maintains peace in us through the works He does through us. We must allow God to work in our heart and mind. We must allow Him to supplant our natural thinking with His supernatural thought patterns. He plans to grant us His perspective and bring us into a deeper life as we walk in His power and peace. This principle is confirmed by Paul:

His presence in our hearts maintains peace in our souls.

> *"And to know the love of Christ, which passeth knowledge,* **that ye might be filled with all the fulness of God.**
>
> *Now unto him that is able to do exceeding abundantly above all that we ask or think, according to the power that worketh in us."* (Ephesians 3:19-20)

God wants to indwell you because He is the great Maintainer of peace. His presence in our hearts maintains peace in our souls. As God works through us, He maintains His peace within us. We must allow Him to bring this peace into our hearts and maintain it within us throughout our lives. The effect this process has on the world around us is powerful. God's peace is part of His witness to the world.

> *"For it is God which **worketh in you both
> to will and to do of his good pleasure**."*
>
> (Philippians 2:13)

Every good work we do is actually the work of God in our lives. God forgives our sins and reconciles us to Himself, then He enables us to do the work which keeps us in His path of peace. This involves walking forgiveness with others and reflecting His character in our everyday lives. It's a wonderful cycle of redemption that touches everyone we know for Jesus. In the next sections, we'll explore that idea further, but first let's learn more about maintaining our peace.

# 6. Peace Is Contingent on Doing What Is Right

> *"But **the meek shall inherit** the earth; and
> **shall delight themselves in the abundance
> of peace**."*        (Psalm 37:11)

This promise is for the meek, who have no anger, and do what is right in the eyes of the Lord. Those who are not ruled by their temper and emotions maintain their peace and *delight* themselves in it. God is telling us that His peace is such a wonderful thing that we will actually be delighted by it. That means that His peace, like His presence, is a source of joy.

That verse also said that we will inherit the earth. What does that mean? It means that everything that needs to happen and come to pass in your favor is going to happen according to the will of God.

> *"In his days* **shall the righteous flourish;**
> **and abundance of peace** *so long as the*
> *moon endureth."* (Psalm 72:7)

God wants the righteous to flourish and live in an everlasting and perfect peace. This promise is only for the righteous—those who choose God and have peace with God. Peace is part of the righteous man's inheritance in Christ and can never be taken away from him.

Our inheritance has a myriad of benefits. Let's look at a few together.

> *"***Great peace have they which love thy***
> **law: and nothing shall offend them***."*
> (Psalm 119:165)

This is a big deal—for all of us! Never to be offended? Jesus gave us clear direction on how to handle offenses. First, Jesus told us to, "Love your enemies...bless those that curse you" (Matt. 5:44). This prevents us from returning evil for evil, ugliness for ugliness. Evil can never conquer evil. That has never worked. If we practice loving our enemies and blessing those who treat us badly, we "overcome evil with good" (Rom. 12:21). God brings us to a place where we can learn to love through Him. This love overcomes offenses. God's love defuses any bomb that threatens to blow up and destroy relationships.

## Jesus loved to forgive.

The crux of the matter is God's command to forgive. Since we have been forgiven, we have the capacity to forgive in the same way. Forgiveness prevents the bitterness that comes from what others may do or say. Do we choose

*14*

to forgive? Do we *love* to forgive? Jesus *loved* to forgive. Through Him, we can too.

> *"For **if ye forgive men** their trespasses, **your heavenly Father will also forgive you**:*
>
> *But if ye forgive **not men** their trespasses, **neither will your Father forgive** your trespasses."* (Matthew 6:14-15)

Imagine that! Walking in forgiveness is the natural outgrowth of loving our Father because forgiveness is the heart of God's love. Conversely, the consequences of *not* loving the law of God to forgive is that we will not be forgiven. Ouch!

Loving the laws of God pleases God to the point that it even affects your enemies:

> *"When a man's ways please the Lord, he maketh **even his enemies** to be at peace with him."* (Proverbs 16:7)

This is the work of righteousness.

God has given His law to direct us in what we should do. When we follow this law, we abide in His great peace. This does not mean that we will never face adversity or never feel afraid, but it does mean that God will support and deliver us in every trial.

> *"And the **work** of righteousness **shall be peace**; and the **effect** of righteousness **quietness and assurance for ever.***
>
> *And **my people shall dwell in a peaceable habitation**, and **in sure dwellings**, and **in quiet resting places**."* (Isaiah 32:17-18)

This passage in Isaiah affirms the psalmist's words which we just considered: *The work of righteousness shall bring peace.* The effect of doing what is right is quietness and assurance—forever. Peace is contingent upon doing what is right.

> *"O that thou hadst hearkened to my commandments!* **then had thy peace been as a river**, *and thy righteousness as the waves of the sea."* (Isaiah 48:18)

Note the pathos in the voice of God in this verse. If we keep the commands of God, we will have peace like a river. God has revealed what we are to do in His Word, and maintains the peace in our hearts that He gives us when we obey Him. God passionately longs for us to have peace.

> *"But the wicked are like the troubled sea, when it cannot rest, whose waters cast up mire and dirt.*
>
> **There is no peace**, *saith my God,* **to the wicked**.*"* (Isaiah 57:20-21)

Make no mistake about it. The wicked are like the troubled seas that toss and turn and have no rest, while the righteous are not driven, but gently led by a Shepherd who loves them and cares for them. Once we know Him, He enables us to follow Him wholly, making choices that honor Him and build our relationship with Him.

Peace can only come when we do what is right. When we do wrong, we lose our peace. Christ has given us peace and promises to maintain that peace; that peace is only withdrawn when we sin.

# 7. Personal Peace Affects All Our Relationships

Your personal peace is not just for your own benefit. It affects all your relationships and interactions. Peace is inward for our hearts and outward towards others. Jesus plainly states:

> *"Salt is good: but if the salt have lost his saltness, wherewith will ye season it?* ***Have salt in yourselves, and have peace one with another.***" (Mark 9:50)

We must have peace with one another. In fact, it must characterize all of our relationships. Remember our definition of peace? Peace is the realm where chaos is not allowed to enter. In this realm, God protects us in our relationships, making them secure and free in Him. We do not want chaos to reign in any of our relationships. God wants us to be at peace with our spouse, our children, our parents, our friends, our business associates—everybody.

> *"****Follow peace with all men****, and holiness, without which no man shall see the Lord:*
>
> ***Looking diligently*** *lest any man fail of the grace of God; lest any root of bitterness springing up trouble you, and thereby many be defiled."* (Hebrews 12:14-15)

Following peace with all men requires *speaking* peacefully to them. If you speak spitefully to others to get a reaction from them, you will harm that relationship, and they will probably respond in kind. Nasty breeds nasty.

Our attitudes toward others should be fueled by a heart of compassion, not judgment. We need to communicate with intelligence and kindness to maintain peace. Since God wants us to live in peace with all men, we should speak and act peacefully towards all people.

**The peace we have as an individual should affect all of our relationships for good.**

The author of Hebrews began with an admonition to seek peace with all men; and then moved on to explain that if we failed in this task, we would stir up bitterness instead. This bitterness would trouble us and all those connected with us. The obvious and better choice is God's path. The peace God offers as we walk with Him changes everything. The peace we have as an individual should affect *all* of our relationships for good.

## 8. Peace Is the Basis of Future Well-being

The peace that Christ gives us and maintains in us is the basis of our well-being, not just now, but for the future as well.

> *"O that ye would altogether hold your peace! and it should be **your wisdom**."*
> (Job 13:5)

Holding your peace brings wisdom. Old timers know what it means to hold your peace. It means to "stay silent and keep quiet" even though you'd really like to share a piece of your mind. This verse urges us to do this, saying it is wisdom. Elsewhere, the Bible even commands us to, "Study to be quiet" (1 Thess. 4:11). Sometimes *not* sharing our every thought is the very best thing we can do. However, wisdom is not the end of the benefits. Look at this promise:

> *"Acquaint now thyself with him, and be at peace:* **thereby good shall come unto thee.** *"* (Job 22:21)

If we know and obey God now, we will have peace now. But that's not just for the present. His peace brings "good" which will come to us in the future. Peace ushers in a future of well-being in which we flourish in Him.

# 9. Abide in Peace

It is one thing to have peace for a moment in life, but it is much more important to remain in a peaceful state throughout your life. God wants us to *abide* in peace. Peace that is fleeting is no peace at all. His will is that we literally dwell in His peace all the time.

> *"I will hear what God the LORD will speak:* **for he will speak peace unto his people,** *and to his saints: but let them not turn again to folly."* (Psalm 85:8)

We do not have to be in doubt about our peace either. God has spoken to us. He gives us all we need to know to maintain peace in our lives. He has promised peace for His people as part of our inheritance, so if we listen to God's Word and heed His call, He will give us His peace. However, if we return to folly, which means going back to our earthly practices of foolish and irrational behavior, and choosing to not love and follow the laws of God, we will lose that peace. His peace is maintained through our connection with Him, which must remain in good operating condition every day.

Jesus painted a vivid picture of this relationship in John 15 when He spoke of Himself as the vine and His people as branches that were obviously connected to Him because they were bearing fruit that reflected that abiding relationship. No matter what happened to them, they drew their life's blood from the vine. In the same manner, we draw our peace from our abiding relationship with God and are able to meet every day nestled in that peace.

Most people think that peace comes from having all their ducks in a row or having tranquility all around them or the absence of trouble. This is why so many do not *understand* the peace of God because it's a peace that does not depend on our circumstances. This inner tranquility doesn't make sense to them. The peace of God maintains heart and mind. It controls our emotions. Here's an illustration:

> During the French war, a train carrying dispatches to the headquarters was compelled to go over sixty miles of very rough track, and reach its destination within an hour. The engineer was the bearer of the dispatches, and his wife and child were in the coach. Every moment threatened to pitch the train over the embankment or over a bridge, and, as it rolled from side to side, leaping at times almost in the air, rushing past stations, the few people inside held their breath and often cried out with terror as they sped along. There was one on that train who knew nothing of their fears and that was the child of the engineer. Happy as a bird, she laughed aloud when asked if she were not afraid, and looked up and answered, "Why, my father is at the engine." A

little later, the engineer came into the car to cheer up his wife and, as he wiped the great drops of sweat from his face, the child leaped into his arms and laid her head upon his bosom, as happy and peaceful as when at home. What a lesson for the children of the heavenly Father![2]

That little girl was completely unafraid, even though she was actually in a perilous situation. She trusted her father to get her safely to her destination. We can do the same.

The Bible even gives us specific instruction about maintaining our peace. Take note of the descriptors of peace in the following Scripture.

> *"And the **peace of God,** which passeth all understanding, **shall keep your hearts and minds** through Christ Jesus. Finally, brethren, whatsoever things are **true**, whatsoever things are **honest**, whatsoever things are **just**, whatsoever things are **pure**, whatsoever things are **lovely**, whatsoever things are **of good report**; if there be any **virtue**, and if there be any **praise**, **think on these things**."* (Philippians 4:7-8)

Again, Philippians 4:7-8 is central to our understanding of peace. As we consider the Lord's exhortation to abide in peace, we need to understand that abiding in peace is key to having good mental health. If our mind (our operating system) is not at peace, our entire lives will be in chaos all the time. We will be prone to crying out in fear like the

---

2       W. M. Tidwell, *Effective Illustrations* (Nicholasville, KY: Schmul Pub. Co., 2010).

people on that train. However, if our minds are stayed on God and trusting in Him (Isa. 26:3)—if we abide in His peace—our hearts and minds will be kept in a state of well-being instead. Jesus will do this.

In this section of Philippians, Paul says we must *think* about certain things to have peace. It is worth our time to examine this list of eight thoughts which should rule our minds.

First, we should think about things that are true. The world tells us that there is no truth, that all things are relative. However, the Bible has a different message altogether. God has revealed absolute truth, and when we think upon His truth, we have peace.

Second, we should think on things that are *honest.* We should not be among those who manipulate or engage in treachery and trickery. We should be forthright and consistent, honest in all our dealings. Further, we should not expose our hearts and minds to lies. Since we grow up surrounded by lies, this is an area in which we need to continually submit our thoughts to God, so He can sift the lies from His truth, and help us grow.

Third, we should think upon things that are *just. Justice* refers to conformity with God's revealed will. Things that are *just* are righteous—those practices God says will please Him. Our thoughts should dwell upon justice.

Fourth, we should think upon things that are *pure.* Impure thoughts bring chaos and darkness into our lives. Purity, however, brings peace. Purity also protects our minds and hearts from the filth of the world we live in. When we think pure thoughts, we're just not on the same page anymore, and we do not engage in anything that does not measure up to God's standard. Instead our minds are tranquil and clean.

Fifth, we should think upon things that are *lovely*. God has given us a good creation in which we live, and it is worthwhile to dwell upon those things in it which are lovely. However, since the fall of mankind, the created world has been corrupted by sin, so that there are now things in it that are unlovely around us too. To maintain peace, we must dwell upon the lovely and shun the unlovely. The good news here is that there is a whole lot of lovely left for us to meditate on. This intentional choosing of the beautiful and the good helps transform our perspective. We begin to see what God sees better when our focus takes into account all He has made.

Sixth, we must think upon things that are of *good report*. Conjecture, gossip, suspicion, and exaggeration are all enemies of peace. Instead of engaging in that kind of talk, we should focus our communication on good reports that are edifying and pleasing to God. We must honestly vet reports that come to us, determining if they are good or bad. Then we shall abide in peace. This habit goes a long way to building one another up and blessing others.

Seventh, our thoughts should dwell upon biblical *virtues*. Charity, diligence, kindness, humility, and patience are all virtues that deserve our time and attention, and benefit us and those around us too.

Finally, Paul tells us to think upon things that are *worthy of praise*. Can we praise God for the thoughts that we are having? If not, we should replace those thoughts with ones that honor Him so we can abide in His peace.

All in all, we are supposed to reflect Jesus to a dying world. Therefore, we should be clearly exhibiting a higher and better way, the path of peace.

If our minds dwell upon the eight ideas outlined in Philippians above: things that are true, honest, just, pure, lovely, of good report, virtuous, and praiseworthy, then we shall dwell in God's peace, and that will be evident to everyone we meet. However, if our thoughts turn to things that lack these virtues, our minds will lack peace and we will open the door to chaos in our lives. It's easy to see how the mental choices we make have a profound effect on our mental health, our witness, and our ability to reach our potential as Christians.

> *"And **let the peace of God rule** in your*
> *hearts, to the which also ye are called in*
> *one body; and be ye thankful."*
> (Colossians 3:15)

In this verse, Paul exhorts us to let the peace of God rule in our hearts. Our hearts and minds should be so infused with peace that every decision, every response, every reaction to anybody and everything, is characterized by peace. Instead of panic and anxiety, we can walk in peace and tranquility. The Scriptures tell us to let peace rule our hearts. We must choose to act out of peace, not anger, anxiety, or panic. Actions ruled by peace will be intelligent, moral, sensible, and wise. If we stay in peace, God will be pleased with our lives and we will be thankful to Him. The *Amplified Version* of this verse gets the point across well. It reads:

> *"And let the peace (**soul harmony** which*
> *comes) from Christ rule (**act as umpire**
> **continually**) in your hearts [**deciding and**
> **settling with finality all questions that**
> **arise in your minds, in that peaceful state**]*
> *to which as [members of Christ's] one*
> *body you were also called [to live]. **And be**
> **thankful** (appreciative), [giving praise to*
> *God always]."* (Colossians 3:15 AMP)

# 10. In Peace, We Must Carry the Message of Peace

True peace is not something reserved for the individual. Those who dwell in God's peace carry this peace into the world around them. We want to carry the message of peace to those who have no peace.

Before turning to Scriptures which explain how this is done, we should first look at a familiar passage which illustrates the danger when we do not carry the message of peace.

> *"And when his brethren saw that their*
> *father loved him more than all his brethren,*
> ***they hated him,*** *and* ***could not speak***
> ***peaceably*** *unto him."*          (Genesis 37:4)

Joseph's brothers were filled with jealousy because their father Jacob loved Joseph more than his other sons. They let this jealousy eat away at their hearts and it turned to hatred. They were unable to speak words of peace and even wanted to kill Joseph. Finally, they sold their own brother into slavery. What drama followed! If you don't know the story, it's really worth reading. It's found in Genesis 39-45.

By now you can see that the stakes are high if we fail to carry the message of peace to others. If we do not, we will miss opportunities and cause unnecessary heartache. It's actually vital that we choose to live in peace. Too often believers go another route, humorously illustrated by Charles Schultz in his beloved Peanuts cartoon strip.

Lucy says to Charlie Brown, "I hate everything. I hate everybody. I hate the whole wide world!"

Charlie says, "But I thought you had inner peace."

Lucy replies, "I do have inner peace. But I still have outer obnoxiousness."[3]

If we do not intentionally practice God's commands in Philippians 4:7-8 and Colossians 3:15 (which we just read on the previous page), we will end up allowing our own version of "outer obnoxiousness" that does not honor our Father or draw others to Him. Instead, we can do real damage to others. This would be a shame in light of what God offers us. Our inner peace is meant to show forth Christ. Our peace has a purpose beyond our own sense of well-being. Peace is a powerful force for good.

> *"**For my brethren and companions' sakes**,*
> *I will now say, Peace be within thee."*
> (Psalm 122:8)

Note that we are to speak peace to others for their sake, not our own. We should be a continual blessing to others once we have received the peace of God. We must experience God's peace in community.

> *"The prophet which prophesieth of peace,*
> *when the word of the prophet shall come to*
> *pass, **then shall the prophet be known, that**
> **the LORD hath truly sent him**."*
> (Jeremiah 28:9)

---

3      Ray Parascando, "Lent: Day 16 Having the Peace of God: February 24, 2016," Crossroads Church, February 26, 2016, https://crossroadsny.org/mydailyinspiration/lent-day-16-peace-god-february-24-2016/.

God clearly shows us the importance of peace by using it as a litmus test for true prophecy. Those who follow the Lord will be persons of peace and righteousness. They will share God's peace with others instead of bringing chaos and confusion to those around them. The Lord sends those who are filled with His peace to share His peace. How do we know if somebody comes in the name of God? We examine their message. If the message is one of peace, we know that they come from God.

> *"And when ye come into an house, salute it.*
>
> *And **if the house be worthy, let your peace come upon it**: but if it be not worthy, let your peace return to you."*
>
> (Matthew 10:12-13)

In these verses Jesus gave instructions to His disciples about how they are to spread the message of peace. He told them to "salute" the houses they enter. But what does this mean?

In Jewish culture, when you entered somebody's house, you would say, "*Shalom!*" which means "Peace be upon you!" They literally spoke peace into their households.

> They literally spoke peace into their households.

This would not only state your peaceful intentions, but also pronounce a blessing on the household that had invited you.

Christ commanded His disciples to do the same, but He did not stop with that. He continued His instruction by telling His disciples to withdraw that blessing from households that were unworthy. Those who reject the blessing of peace in the gospel cannot experience peace in their lives. The disciples could not force God's peace upon those who were unwilling to receive it, and Jesus was telling them that they should not be troubled when this happens because their peace rested in Him instead of those who rejected His message. They would abide in peace even when people rejected and reviled them. The same is true for us today.

> *"And into whatsoever house ye enter, first say, Peace be to this house.*
>
> *And if the son of peace be there, your peace shall rest upon it: if not, it shall turn to you again."* (Luke 10:5-6)

The parallel passage in Luke tells us the same principle.

## Summing Up

The gospel of Jesus Christ should give us peace. The incarnation, crucifixion, and resurrection of our Lord is the core of that gospel. If we embrace this gospel, we will have peace with God, with ourselves, and with others. This promise of peace brings us hope even in our darkest moments. If we accept this gospel, we will become messengers of peace to a world that is plagued with chaos. The peace that indwells us will carry into every aspect of our lives forever as long as we abide in it and characterize each of our relationships. It will affect all our activities. Without this gospel, the opposite will be true: We will be bereft of peace in our hearts and minds, and plagued with anxiety and chaos instead. It is my prayer that you will know God's peace, abide in it, and share it with others. Because others will recognize God's peace in you, they will want to know how you got that way, and you will be able to share the good news of this precious gift of peace with them. If you know Jesus and His peace, you can change the world.

# Chapter 2

# The Way to Genuine Peace

G enuine peace must be our core condition. Without it, we will be unable to make wise decisions, enjoy positive relationships, or maintain our mental health. Many people have a false peace or a fleeting one. That's not good enough. Each of us needs genuine, long-lasting peace.

Perhaps you have heard the old joke, "I'm so used to being anxious that when I start to get calm, I get nervous." I hope this is not true of you, but if it is, these next chapters will help you find genuine lasting peace.

## 1. Anything Fake Is Dangerous

The first thing we must understand is that anything fake is dangerous—to ourselves and others. Our world is brimming with the deceitful, the underhanded, the superficial, the false. Let's look at some Scriptures that clarify the dangers involved in these choices.

> ***"Thou shalt not bear false witness*** *against thy neighbour."*　　　(Exodus 20:16)

Truth is so fundamental to morality that God addressed it in the Ten Commandments. He very plainly stated that we must not lie; we must not bear false witness against anybody. Without truth, there can be no morality. Just a few chapters later, Moses repeated God's command:

> *"**Thou shalt not raise a false report**: put not thine hand with the wicked to be an unrighteous witness.*
>
> ***Thou shalt not follow a multitude to do evil**; neither shalt thou speak in a cause to decline after many to wrest judgment."*
> (Exodus 23:1-2)

Just a few chapters later, Moses repeated this again. He maintained that giving a false report aligned a person with the wicked. A deceitful witness is actually choosing to side against the Lord! Moses warned that even if it seemed as though everyone around us was deceitful, that was no excuse to join them in that practice. Just because we are surrounded by liars and a culture of lies built on a throne of lies does not make it acceptable to lie. We must embrace truth and not be caught in the same practices as the wicked.

> *"**Deliver my soul**, O LORD, **from lying lips**, and from **a deceitful tongue**.*
>
> *What shall be given unto thee? or what shall be done unto thee, thou false tongue?"*
> (Psalm 120:2-3)

In this verse, the psalmist asked the Lord to deliver him from deceit. Knowing God is a God of truth, he chose to trust God to deliver him from the dangers of falsehood. We too can turn to the Lord when we are confronted by those who would hurt us with their lies. We can find shelter in Him, and trust Him for deliverance. Liars seek to hurt and destroy. They try to build themselves up by bringing others down. They are a dangerous threat, but the God of truth is stronger.

> *"**A false balance** is abomination to the LORD: but a just weight is his delight."*
> (Proverbs 11:1)

A false balance refers to inaccurate scales used to cheat people. For instance, a gas station pump registers how much gas you receive from it. A "false balance" in this context would claim to have put a full gallon in your car when it only delivered a three-quarters of a gallon, thereby cheating you of a quarter gallon for every gallon you pumped from it. This proverb warns against false dealings in our economic relationships. We should not cheat others, and should be on guard against those who would cheat us.

> *"**Most men will proclaim** every one **his own goodness**: but a faithful man who can find?"*
> (Proverbs 20:6)

This proverb urges us to be wise in the face of one who loudly proclaims his or her righteousness. If a person is truly good, they will be humble about their obedience. They will recognize that their goodness is a gift from God, and that they have no reason to boast about it. People who boast that they are good, usually are not.

*"**Whoso boasteth himself of a false gift is like clouds and wind without rain**."*
(Proverbs 25:14)

Boasters surround us. People puffed up in their own pride are everywhere. Their goal is to trick people into thinking highly of them with their bragging, but they are like a false gift. They believe they are special and that you are blessed to know them, but they are no better than a cloud that can't deliver any rain. They are, in fact, useless, and spend their time in pointless pursuits. Even Aesop had something to say about the proud and the boastful:

A certain man who visited foreign lands could talk of little when he returned to his home except the wonderful adventures he had met with and the great deeds he had done abroad. One of the feats he told about was a leap he had made in a city called Rhodes. That leap was so great, he said, that no other man could leap anywhere near the distance. A great many persons in Rhodes had seen him do it and would prove that what he told was true.

"No need of witnesses," said one of the hearers. "Suppose this city is Rhodes. Now show us how far you can jump."

Deeds count, not boasting words.[4]

Unfortunately, not all are so obvious as the one described above. Too often others are taken in by the seeming confidence of a braggart, but they're not fooling God, and thankfully, God protects those who seek after Him.

---

4        Aesop, "The Boasting Traveler," Fables of Aesop, November 23, 2020, https://fablesofaesop.com/the-boasting-traveler.html.

*"There is a generation that are **pure in their own eyes**, and yet is **not washed** from their filthiness.*

*There is a generation, O how lofty are their eyes! and their eyelids are lifted up."*

(Proverbs 30:12-13)

Those who *knowingly* embrace that which is not genuine are themselves frauds. They are cheaters, deceivers, counterfeiters, hoaxers, shams, and pretenders. They are haughty, looking as though they are lifting their eyes to heaven, while their hearts are full of artificial piety and insincerity. They are proud of their imagined purity, but are filthy in reality. God warns us not to trust in such people.

A good example of this would be the two men in the temple in Luke 18:9-14. The humble man would not even look up to heaven as he prayed, but begged for help while the boastful man proudly told God all he had done for Him, as if God was lucky to have him as His child. Jesus said the first man was heard by God, not the second. God knows the truth about every person, so it is a futility to try to put one over on Him. And He is the One in the end that matters. The boastful really care nothing for God. Their agenda is set on what they can gain in the here and now through trickery and deceit. But that's not the path God calls us to follow.

He encourages us to pursue genuine peace in Him instead and let Him extend that peace into our relationships with others. God in His wisdom has lovingly given us this warning and encouragement to keep us from danger.

*"**Folly is set in great dignity**, and the rich sit in low place."*     (Ecclesiastes 10:6)

33

*Folly* in this passage refers to shameful things, silly things—things that are not genuine. Our culture applauds such, but we know they are not valued in the sight of God.

> *"Behold,* **I am against them that prophesy false dreams***, saith the LORD, and do tell them, and cause my people to err by their lies, and by their lightness; yet I sent them not, nor commanded them:* **therefore they shall not profit this people** *at all, saith the LORD."* (Jeremiah 23:32)

The prophet Jeremiah condemned those who spoke falsely in the name of the Lord. It is particularly loathsome when deceivers claim to speak the truth in God's name, but are really spreading lies. Not only does this dishonor God, but it also can lead others astray and cause them grief. False prophets may use words of flattery to try to deceive their listeners, but these words can only lead to harm.

> *"Woe unto you, when all men shall speak well of you! for so did their fathers to the* **false prophets***."* (Luke 6:26)

Jeremiah was not the only one to warn us against false prophets. Jesus cautioned us to be wary of flatterers. False prophets tell you what they think you want to hear instead of the truth. They do not tell you what you *need* to hear, but tickle your ears with flattering words instead. The motivation of their hearts is crooked.

False prophets are surely dangerous because they can lead you astray, but false friends are just as bad. False friends will betray us in the end, which can cause disillusionment in our inner core. This is why it is so important that we be strongly connected to the Lord. Jesus experienced the pain and loss that comes with investing in a relationship that did not turn out well. In Him, we can find comfort and direction when this happens to us.

The apostle Paul knew that false friends fueled by their own ulterior motives represented a great danger too.

> *"In journeyings often, in perils of waters, in perils of robbers, in perils by mine own countrymen, in perils by the heathen, in perils in the city, in perils in the wilderness, in perils in the sea, **in perils among false brethren."*** (2 Corinthians 11:26)

David also experienced the pain of false friends:

> *"For it was not an enemy that reproached me; then I could have borne it: neither was it he that hated me that did magnify himself against me; then I would have hid myself from him:*
>
> ***But it was thou, a man mine equal, my guide, and mine acquaintance.***
>
> *We took sweet counsel together, and walked unto the house of God in company."*
> (Psalm 55:12-14)

David wrote that it was not an enemy who reproached him, mocked him, made fun of him, and told everybody he was stupid. If it had been an enemy, David would have expected that kind of treatment, and been able to bear it better. That's what enemies do. But it was not an enemy who treated David cruelly. It was someone he considered a true friend. It was someone with whom he worshiped and whose counsel he had trusted. There may be no greater pain than knowing that somebody you loved and trusted has betrayed you, but it happens very often. Spouses betray each other, families split apart, and friends treat each other unkindly. David's intimate friend claimed to be a fellow believer.

Counterfeit believers fill our churches today. They are people who claim to follow Christ, but do not. This can be depressing, but we must remember that counterfeits are also proof that the genuine exist. You will never come across a counterfeit three-dollar bill because a three-dollar bill has never been printed. On the other hand, you might encounter a counterfeit twenty as we actually have those in circulation. We would never throw away *all* our twenty-dollar bills because someone is printing phony ones. Anyone who throws away real twenties because someone is printing phony ones is beyond foolish. In the same way, we should not reject being a Christian just because there are phony ones; most certainly, we should never cease being genuine friends because others are not. Even though Jesus knew what Judas would do, He never rejected him. Even though we are aware of how dangerous and painful it is to be betrayed, we must still choose to love others and look for genuine friends in the body of Christ.

> *"Even so **ye also outwardly appear**
> **righteous unto men**, but within ye are full
> of hypocrisy and iniquity."*
> (Matthew 23:28)

Outward appearances can be deceiving. A person might look like a believer, but be corrupt on the inside. The Bible warns us to be on guard against such hypocrites. They are narcissists, only interested in advancing themselves at the expense of others. They are playing god because they do not have a sincere love for Him in the first place. They consider themselves superior to others and are hurtful to those around them in their arrogant disregard.

Nothing can disturb the peace in your life faster than false friends and hypocrites. They bring chaos, anxiety, and heartache in their wake. God wants you to live in peace, so once you identify these purveyors of deceit, it is best to stay away from them. They will only attempt to destroy your peace.

# 2. Fake Peace Debilitates Us

> *"Draw me not away with the wicked, and with the workers of iniquity, which **speak peace** to their neighbours, **but mischief is in their hearts."*** (Psalm 28:3)

False peace hurts us and those with whom we have relationships. David pleads with God to keep wicked people away from him. The wicked pretend to speak peace, but their hearts are full of evil intent. They speak false peace.

In Scripture, God tenderly cares for His people just as a good father loves his daughter. In Jeremiah, the people of Israel had come under God's judgment for their disobedience. False teachers and prophets were giving Israel false hope and telling them that God was going to give them peace when God was actually saying something completely different.

People who say there is peace when there is no true peace deceive others as well as themselves. They bring a false sense of security to the vulnerable and take advantage of them. False peace leaves people confused and anxious. It also damages our minds, so that we cannot make wise decisions.

# 3. Authentic Peace Is Priceless

> *"Mark the perfect man, and behold, the upright: for **the end of that man is peace.**"*
> (Psalm 37:37)

The reward of a good life is peace. The Bible does not tell us that our reward is great riches or good health. Our reward is not something the world regards as valuable like gold or silver. God knows that peace is more valuable than any amount of money, so that is His gift to us.

> *"For the mountains shall depart, and the hills be removed; but my kindness shall not depart from thee, **neither shall the covenant of my peace be removed**, saith the Lord that hath mercy on thee."*
> (Isaiah 54:10)

Very few things in life are solid and certain. We can lose our job, our health, our money, even our lives or the lives of our loved ones. However, in all that, we know that if we have Christ, we can never lose God's peace. Isaiah reminds us that God will never remove His covenant of peace from His people.

Things that last are more valuable than things that fall apart. If you had a choice between a car that you could rely on for five years and one that would last fifteen years, you would choose the one that ran fifteen years. God's gift of peace is much better than that. Authentic peace is priceless because it lasts *forever*.

> *"For the kingdom of God is not meat and drink; but righteousness, **and peace**, and joy in the Holy Ghost.*
>
> *For he that in these things serveth Christ is acceptable to God, and approved of men.*
>
> ***Let us therefore follow after the things which make for peace**, and things wherewith one may edify another."*
>
> (Romans 14:17-19)

Paul reminds us that God's kingdom is not about carnal pleasures like eating and drinking. God's kingdom is about spiritual realities such as righteousness, joy, and peace. Our salvation grants us what we really need. We really need peace. God's peace is far more valuable than anything the world has to offer.

> Authentic peace is priceless because it lasts forever.

As a young person, I would probably not have placed peace high on my list of needs, but as I grew older I recognized the profound value of having peace within my soul. Today I treasure that peace more than any possession or position, because I have learned that I can rely on the peace of God in any trying circumstance that will come my way. More on that later.

# 4. There Are Only Two Kinds of Peace: True Peace and False Peace

> *"**Peace I leave with you, my peace I give unto you: not as the world giveth**, give I unto you. Let not your heart be troubled, neither let it be afraid."*　(John 14:27)

Jesus promised His followers that He would leave them with His peace. He explained that the peace He would give them is different from the kind of peace the world offers. These two concepts of peace are diametrically opposed to one another. Those who abide in the peace of Jesus need not be afraid or troubled; their hearts can rest in His hope and peace. Those that rely on the world for peace may lose what they think they possess at any given moment because it is not a real or lasting peace.

> *"**Beware lest any man spoil you through philosophy and vain deceit**, after the tradition of men, after the rudiments of the world, and not after Christ."*
>
> (Colossians 2:8)

Since God loves us and wants us to live in His peace, He cautions us about anything that can rob our peace. This is one of the ways He shows His love for us. He wants to keep us safe and protected. The verse you just read is just one of these warnings.

Paul warns us that the philosophies of the world are vain and deceitful. The world cannot give us peace. The traditions of men present worldviews that are opposed to Christ and the true path to peace. These competing worldviews will confuse you if you let them. Worldviews are the basis for the way we think and view the world around us. Since our ideas have consequences, if our worldview is marred or impaired, our decisions will be negatively affected.

A faulty worldview will bring your heart and mind into chaos instead of restful peace in the end. Many believe that the wisdom of this world has the capacity to solve all of humanity's problems, but Paul says that these hopes can only be disappointed. There are only two options: God's way and the world's. God's path leads to true peace and well-being, while the world's winding trails lead to false peace and despair, even though they loudly claim the reverse. Once again, we can think back to the boastful fools that arrogantly follow their own perverse ways and think they will not founder, but will end well. This is not the case.

> *A faulty worldview will bring your heart and mind into chaos instead of restful peace.*

> *"The way of a fool is right in his own eyes: but he that hearkeneth unto counsel is wise."* (Proverbs 12:15)

Fools do not perceive their own foolishness. They believe that they are right. Wicked people believe that their wicked deeds are justified. In the stubbornness of their own hearts, they follow the path that seems best to them. Nevertheless, their works will not lead them to lasting peace. Only those who are wise and follow God's path to peace will find what their hearts need.

*"**Every way of a man is right in his own***
***eyes**: but the LORD pondereth the hearts."*
(Proverbs 21:2)

This proverb teaches us something very similar to the previous one. Sinful man is not even aware of his own folly. He is right in his own eyes. He thinks he has peace, but his peace is not genuine. God's way to peace is not man's way to peace. These two worldviews are incompatible.

*"The **way of peace they know not**; and*
*there is no judgment in their goings: they*
*have made them crooked paths: whosoever*
*goeth therein shall **not know peace**."*
(Isaiah 59:8)

The world does not know peace. In fact, the Personnel Journal, a periodical devoted to understanding resource management, reported this incredible statistic: Since the beginning of recorded history, the entire world has been at peace *less than eight percent of the time!* In its study, the periodical discovered that of 3,530 years of recorded history, only 286 years saw peace. Moreover, in excess of 8,000 peace treaties were made—and broken.[5] That's pretty pitiful. The world has no grasp on the concept of peace, and never has.

Many people who follow the world's version of peace cannot exercise good judgment, so they make poor life decisions as a result. Their cacophony of ideologies and philosophies are altogether crooked. As they follow the world's ways, they make poor decisions and find themselves walking on a treacherous and difficult path. As

---

5      Moody Bible Institute's Today in the Word, June, 1988, p. 33.

they stumble along, the last thing they will find on that crooked way is peace. Instead they will struggle to make reasonable decisions. In the end, only disaster awaits them. And it doesn't matter how "successful" they may look at any juncture. They are only investing in a worldly existence while their eternal life is in peril—a problem of which they are unaware. That's how well their human wisdom serves them in the end.

Human wisdom cannot attain real peace. That can only come from God and requires following the path He has laid out for us. His peace is so important that it frames the entire passage just quoted from Isaiah. Note that it begins with the phrase: "The way of peace they know not," and ends with "whosoever goeth therein shall not know peace." Isaiah is saying that the way of God's peace is of paramount importance. Anyone whose path does not follow this way is in serious trouble, whether they realize it or not.

> *"**Destruction and misery are in their ways**:*
> *And the way of peace have they not known:*
> *There is **no fear of God** before their eyes."*
> (Romans 3:16-18)

Paul picks up this same theme in Romans: Those who do not fear God shall not know peace. Their fate is destruction and misery. They do not know how to escape that fate because they are relying on their own wisdom and sense of false peace. They are incapable of making wise, moral decisions. Peace is *not* in their hearts. They think they know the way of peace, but their wisdom is foolishness in the eyes of God. Man naturally thinks that he is wiser than God; in reality, this is foolishness. How can a finite man be wiser than the infinite God? How can the creature be wiser than the Creator? God is all-wise and the Source of all wisdom. Without God, man has no wisdom and cannot find peace.

# 5. God's Way Surpasses Natural Understanding

> *"And the peace of God, **which passeth all understanding**, shall keep your hearts and minds through Christ Jesus."*
>
> (Philippians 4:7)

Let's revisit our key passage again. How can we grasp something which is beyond our ability to understand? As mentioned earlier, to "understand" is to be able to explain the logic of why things happen and make sense of the world around us. Simply put, understanding is the ability to see cause and effect. If I pay my electric bill, the power company will give me electricity. If I hit my thumb with a hammer, I will get a bruise. We can easily grasp the cause and effect in these actions.

## We are tethered to God's peace.

Our understanding of this process is fine in these simple illustrations, but breaks down when it comes to larger, more global and abstract ideas, like true peace.

The world views peace as a feeling or an emotion, and applies cause and effect to this idea. The world tells us that if we take a particular action or travel in a certain way, we will have peace in our lives. Their version of peace is contingent on something we do, and dependent on our life's circumstances.

This is not how God's peace works. God's peace is a gift to us and is not dependent on our circumstances or our feelings. It is not built upon how things are going. God's peace does not follow the world's pattern of cause and effect. Instead it is beyond our understanding; and since it is His gift, nobody can take it away from us.

God's peace will guard our hearts and minds in Christ Jesus. If God's peace is the core condition of our hearts, then we do not need to worry about our mental health. No matter what our circumstances are, we will be able to rest in Him. We will not have to worry about the decisions we make either because we are resting in His peace and directed by Him.

Because it is the underpinning of our hearts, we will not be ruled by anger or prone to making rash decisions. God's peace enables us to be meek, and it is the meek who will inherit the earth. We are not slaves to our circumstances. Instead, we can abide in hopeful peace, knowing that God loves us and will take care of us—whether things are going well or not. We cannot control our circumstances or what goes on in the world around us, and this lack of control sometimes feels frightening, but we are tethered to God's peace, so we do not need to be afraid. As I write this, the world is facing a terrible virus that is out of our control. I cannot stop the virus, but I can still know God's peace which will keep me stable, healthy, mentally alert, and uncontaminated by the avalanche of negative news around me. This is true for any problem—no matter how large or small. The peace of God will keep your heart and understanding.

# 6. Jesus Is the Only Way to Genuine Peace

This point is the crux of the issue. Believers know what true peace is, and that God is the only Source of that peace. The question is: How do we get true everlasting peace from

God? The answer lies in the life and work of Jesus Christ. He is the only way to genuine peace.

> *"To* **give knowledge of salvation unto his people by the remission of their sins,**
>
> *Through the tender mercy of our God; whereby the dayspring from on high hath visited us.*
>
> *To give light to them that sit in darkness and in the shadow of death,* **to guide our feet into the way of peace."**
>
> (Luke 1:77-79)

We have already mentioned the reasons why Christ came to earth. Here Luke repeats that reason: Christ came to give knowledge of salvation to His people by the remission of their sins. Remission refers to complete and total forgiveness. It may seem impossible that God could completely erase our sin, but that is what He has done.

## Never doubt that the God who can create something out of nothing, can also create nothing out of something.

Never doubt that the God who can create something out of nothing, can also create nothing out of something. God is all-powerful. As the Master of the Universe, He created the entire universe *out of nothing.* This same God who created all things out of nothing can completely erase your sins. He can render every portion of your sin into nothing at all. In fact, He does more than that.

He takes our sin—all of it—upon Himself, and then, He counts us as righteous in His sight. God does not look at us as sinners. He only sees the perfect righteousness of His Son who knew no sin. Our sin no longer rules us. It no longer defines us. It cannot trouble us. Our past does not define our future. This is why Christ came. This great exchange saves us. Our sins are forgiven and left behind. We are righteous in God's sight. This should encourage and give us peace. God gives us the knowledge of salvation and forgiveness of our sins, establishing us in His perfect peace.

Luke refers to Jesus as the Dayspring from on high. Jesus' coming to earth represented a new dawning, a new day which brought new light and hope to a fallen world. God did not send forth His Son in wrath to visit judgment and destruction upon us for our sin. Instead, God, in His tender mercy, sent the "dayspring from on high" to visit us and live with us, fully God and fully man. Jesus came to show us the way of true peace and forgiveness.

Most people in the world do not understand the meaning of life. They stumble about in darkness because they do not follow Christ. Christ is the only One who can give us light, so He can guide us into this peace. While the world is stumbling towards death, Jesus lives to saves us from that end.

> *"Thomas saith unto him, Lord, we know not whither thou goest; and how can we know the way?*
>
> *Jesus saith unto him, **I am the way, the truth, and the life**: no man cometh unto the Father, but by me."*  (John 14:5-6)

This passage is part of Jesus' "farewell discourse." The gospel of John gives us the most detailed account of all that Jesus told His disciples before He went to the cross.

Jesus knew what was coming. He knew Judas would betray Him, Peter would deny Him, and Thomas would doubt Him. He knew His disciples would flee in fear, stricken with doubt and despair. Instead of chastising them for their lack of faith, He provided them with words of comfort and encouragement—words that still bring us comfort and encouragement today.

Doubting Thomas still did not understand the gospel at this point and questioned Jesus about the way to follow Him. Jesus explained that He is the way. He is the way to God, to heaven, to peace. There is no other way. He is the way, so we shall never be lost. He is the truth, so we shall never be paralyzed with confusion. He is the life, so when faced with hopeless depression and despair, we will not be overcome by it.

# 7. God's Thoughts about You Are Peaceful

Imagine if you could somehow look inside the mind of God. Believe it or not, you would see *you*! God thinks about you. He is a God of loving-kindness who cares for His creatures. Most people do not realize that God thinks about them. What kinds of thoughts does God have about us? Thoughts of peace! Wow!

> *"**How precious also are thy thoughts unto me**, O God! **how great is the sum of them**!*
>
> *If I should count them, they are more in number than the sand: when I awake, I am still with thee."*          (Psalm 139:17-18)

Imagine you have a handful of sand. How many grains would you be holding? Hundreds? Thousands? Probably around 10,000 grains of sand just in your hand! David says that the sum of God's thoughts is greater than not just the grains of sand you could hold in your hand, but greater than *all* the sand that exists worldwide. Think about that! All the hundreds of thousands of miles of seashore, all the sand at the bottom of the ocean, all the great sand dunes of the deserts and coastlands. God's thoughts are infinitely greater than the total number of all those grains of sand!

> *"As for me, since I am poor and needy, **let the Lord keep me in his thoughts.** You are my helper and my savior. O my God, do not delay."*　　　　　(Psalm 40:17)

Amazingly, even with all those thoughts, God has a special place in His mind for you and me. He keeps us in His thoughts. That means that right now, He is thinking about you. His divine thoughts are thoughts of peace— peace with Him forever. He never leaves us alone, even for a moment, but is a continual source of encouragement and hope, a well that never runs dry. No one else is more worthy of all of our love and affection.

> *"For I know the thoughts that I think toward you, saith the LORD, **thoughts of peace**, and not of evil, **to give you an expected end."***　　　(Jeremiah 29:11)

Jeremiah corroborates the fact that God's thoughts about us are peaceful. God is not cruel, waiting for the next opportunity to punish us in some way. He is a loving Father who wants us to experience and walk in His peace throughout our lives. How often does the Lord have these thoughts about us? Are we just a fleeting thought in the mind of God or does He deeply care for us? Psalm 40 has this to say:

> *"I am poor and needy;* **yet the Lord**
> **thinketh upon me***: thou art my help and my*
> *deliverer; make no tarrying, O my God."*
>
> (Psalm 40:17)

# 8. God Is a Peacemaker

God does not seek to bring trouble to His created order. He wants people to know peace, and He wants His creation to be at peace. Some people believe that God brings trouble to the world or that religious belief is a source of violence, but the Bible says this is not true. It tells us that our God is a peaceful God. Here's an example:

In the late 1800s, Amy Carmichael, a young Irish girl, began serving as a missionary in India. She remained there without leave for over 55 years. At some point in her service, she began rescuing young girls who had been sold to the temple priests, where they lived lives of "moral and spiritual danger." Little girls were not valued in Indian society; and if a family was very poor, they often sold girls into lives of servitude, or dedicated them to the temples in an effort to get a blessing from one of the many Indian gods and goddesses. These girls lived hard lives and were often exploited. They were drawn to Amy because she loved them, and Amy braved great persecution to champion their cause and keep them from the temple authorities.

It was a situation in which she had to hold to the direction and wisdom of God in spite of the turbulence and threats around her. Amy Carmichael wrote many books and tracts, and in her writings is this simple statement:

> Blessed are the single-hearted, for they shall enjoy much peace. If you refuse to be hurried and pressed, if you stay your soul on God, nothing can keep you from that clearness of spirit which is life and peace. In that stillness you will know what His will is.[6]

Amy Carmichael knew God's peace. She knew that God wanted to bring peace and joy to these little girls who had no hope, and she lived in clarity about God's will. We can do the same. This is hugely important if we are to accomplish the works Jesus has planned for us in our lives. He actually leads us through peaceful pathways.

> *"Now **the God of peace be with you all.**
> Amen."*                    (Romans 15:33)

Paul is saying that God's presence brings peace. Sin is the cause of strife, not God. Wherever God is present, there is peace. When people try to escape from God, they experience turmoil. In their pride, they blame their troubled state on God when it is actually the result of their own choice to reject Him.

> *"Those things, which ye have both learned,
> and received, and heard, and seen in me,*

---

6        "A Biography of Amy Carmichael, Missionary to India," RSS, accessed February 14, 2021, http://missionaryportal.webflow.io/biography/ amy-carmichael#:~:text=Amy%20Carmichael%20Quotes,which%20is%20 life%20and%20peace.

*do:* ***and the God of peace shall be with
you.***"                                  (Philippians 4:9)

God promises to be with us and bring us peace. In
the above verse, Paul admonished the church in Philippi
to heed his words. Paul had taught them how they should
act in the world by word and example. He knew that if
they followed the Lord, God would bring them into perfect
peace. God's peace is a manifestation of His presence.

# 9. Genuine Peace Requires the Knowledge of God

It is not enough to academically understand everything
we have just said in this chapter. Genuine peace requires
that you *know* God. We must know Him personally and
be known by Him personally. We must have a saving
relationship with Him that can only come through Christ.

> *"To give light to them that sit in darkness
> and in the shadow of death, **to guide our
> feet into the way of peace.**"*     (Luke 1:79)

The Bible often uses the metaphor of light to describe
*knowledge*. This indicates that it is not mere head
knowledge, but knowledge that transforms the heart and
illuminates it. According to Luke, Christ came to earth to
give us light, and His light transforms our lives and leads
us into the path of peace.

> *"For **he is our peace**, who hath made both
> one, and hath broken down the middle wall
> of partition between us."* (Ephesians 2:14)

Jesus is our peace. It is not enough to have a superficial, surface knowledge of Christ. We must have a deep personal relationship with Him to have His peace. This point cannot be overemphasized. One writer put it this way:

> For some Christians, a relationship with Jesus consists of praying to Him and going to church on Sunday. They allow Jesus to be a sacrifice for their sins, but the relationship with Him stops there. For others, Jesus is an example to follow, and they try their best to live as He did. But since Jesus is in heaven and they are here, they don't really expect to have much of a relationship with Him, and therefore, in fact, do not. Such relationships with Jesus can, at best, be described as "distant." The Bible, however, speaks about an intimate and dynamic relationship with Jesus. He is, after all, a *person*, not a "theological concept"; not someone who once lived on the earth and now is far away, but a person who is alive and can be very near.[7]

Jesus wants to be our constant companion, one we interact with on a daily basis. When our relationship with Him is deep and intimate, He is able to closely work in our lives, bringing us to a deep level of peace and stability in Him. When Jesus is our peace, He will break down any divisions that exist between His people. He gives us peace with God and peace with one another.

---

7      Vern Nicolette, "How Can I Have a Deeper Relationship with Jesus? John 14:21-23," ActiveChristianity, December 13, 2016, https://activechristianity.org/how-can-i-have-a-deeper-relationship-with-jesus.

> ***"Grace and peace be multiplied unto you***
> *through the knowledge of God, and of Jesus*
> *our Lord."* (2 Peter 1:2)

The apostle Peter said that God will multiply our grace and peace. How? He does it by giving us knowledge of Himself and Jesus. This is not just knowledge about God. It is knowledge that also comes from God. This knowledge is a requirement for grace and peace. I could read about George Washington and say that I know him, but I will never know George Washington in the same way that I know a family member. I have a personal relationship with my family member that I could never have with Washington. The same is true about God. I could read a book about God and say that I know Him, but if I do not have a personal relationship with Him, I will never truly know Him, and I will not be able to abide in His peace.

# 10. Genuine Peace Requires Jesus' Governance

Genuine peace begins with making Jesus the Governor of our life. He must be our Lord. He must be in charge for us to have true peace. If we insist upon our own autonomy, we will not have peace. If we follow the philosophies of this world, we will not have peace. If we do what other people tell us to do, we will not have peace. If we put ourselves in charge instead of God, we will not have peace. Instead, we must yield control of our lives to the Prince of Peace, and He will keep us in His peace. His management and governance is perfect. He has our best interests at heart. When we give Him control, He guides us into everlasting peace. This submission is the first and most important step towards peace.

*"For unto us a child is born, unto us a son is given: and **the government shall be upon his shoulder**: and his name shall be called Wonderful, Counsellor, the mighty God, the everlasting Father, **the Prince of Peace**."*

(Isaiah 9:6)

This is a popular passage to read around Christmas, but it is vital to our study. Isaiah foretold the coming of Jesus, the Messiah. When Isaiah wrote that the government shall be upon His shoulder, he did not mean that Jesus would come and be a head of state. Chrisitanity is a change of government... from self government to Christ's government. Instead of narcissism (selfishness and dominating egos) we bring in a trustworthy management system.

> We must yield control of our lives to the Prince of Peace,

Life Management requires a Manager who loves us supremely and is smart enough to guide us in right paths. His "kingdom" is not a political organization but a new grouping of persons under the the finest of life management systems. Thus, 'the government shall be upon His shoulders.' Additionally, it shows that Jesus must govern our lives.

However, Isaiah goes further by sharing some of Jesus' titles: Wonderful, Counselor, the Mighty God, and the Prince of Peace. Let's focus on this last title: the *Prince* of Peace. A prince is the top-ranking official. He is in charge. Peace must come through Him. Who is in charge of your life? Does the world govern you? Do other people govern you through their opinions? Do you try to govern yourself? The Bible tells us that Jesus must govern us. Most often, the problem is yourself. We put "I" in charge. This little letter causes a great deal of trouble. It is in the middle of the word *pride* and shows up three times in the word *iniquity*. If we put ourselves in charge, we will not have peace.

> *"Of the increase of his government and*
> *peace there **shall be no end**, upon the*
> *throne of David, and upon his kingdom, to*
> *order it, and to establish it with judgment*
> *and with justice from henceforth even for*
> *ever. The zeal of the LORD of hosts will*
> *perform this."*          (Isaiah 9:7)

Isaiah continues by saying that Christ's government will not end. His peace will not end. When we turn our lives over to Christ, we shall know no end to peace. We have joined His kingdom. He reigns upon the throne of David and has established His kingdom with justice forever. His judgment is perfect. He does not have the capacity to make a mistake. His perfect justice and judgment will bring peace. Isaiah reminds us of the certainty of this promise, saying that the zeal of the Lord will accomplish it. He never fails or breaks His promises.

> *"All we like sheep have gone astray; we*
> *have turned every one to his own way; and*
> ***the LORD hath laid on him the iniquity of***
> ***us all.***"          (Isaiah 53:6)

All of us need to be governed by Christ. We are lost sheep without Him. We are full of iniquity. Sheep without a shepherd have no peace. They are isolated. We cannot have peace apart from Christ. God placed all our iniquity on this Good Shepherd. When we follow Him, we have peace. Instead of foolish sheep that are easy prey, we come under the governance of a mighty Shepherd-King and are ushered into His kingdom as sons and daughters. He grants us access to Himself and all He has to offer. Jesus' kingdom is unlike any earthly one, but is unusual in that we never have to fend for ourselves within it.

> *"But he answered and said, It is written,*
> **Man shall not live by bread alone, but**
> **by every word that proceedeth out of the**
> **mouth of God."** (Matthew 4:4)

Most of us are concerned with our physical needs. We worry about our finances, food, our home, and our health, but Matthew reminds us that we do not live on bread alone. Our physical needs are important, but they are not as important as the wisdom, encouragement, guidance, and correction we get from God. We can trust Him. He will never lead us astray or leave us alone. He loves us, and knows what is best for us in every situation. He is the only One with enough wisdom to lead us in peace.

# Summing Up

We have examined the way to genuine peace, and understood the danger inherent in false peace, so by now you can appreciate the importance of authenticity. Since God alone is the Source of true peace, we must truly know God and give Him complete control over our lives to walk in His peace. Take the time to look at your relationship with Jesus today. Do you connect with Him daily or is He distant in your life? Do you live with a continual sense of His presence with you? If you do not, do two things: First and foremost, pray and ask Him for help in this area. Next, find a Christian, someone you know who has a strong and intimate relationship with Jesus and talk with them. You will know them, not by their speech but by the spiritual fruit in their lives. If you are around a real Christian, you should sense the love of Christ through them. You should feel accepted by them. They will not be perfect, but God's grace should be evident in their lives.

We will continue to look at God's path to genuine peace according to His Word, and see how this peace transforms all our relationships across the board.

# Chapter 3

# Footsteps to Genuine Peace

P eace is one of the most important aspects of life and the foundation of mental health. It enables us to make wise decisions without the interference of outside emotions or circumstances. We have already learned that the difference between the world's way to peace and God's is that the world's way depends upon external circumstances, while God's depends strictly on the condition of the *inside* of a person. In this chapter, we will examine the paths that bring us genuine peace.

We know that God has provided us peace through Christ and that we must maintain that peace. In this chapter, we will see how God's peace causes us to triumph and leads us to an even deeper peace. We will see the role that the Bible, prayer, God's wisdom, and the Holy Spirit play in maintaining it. Finally, we will look at how we are to stay at peace with everyone and how peace should remain the focus of our lives.

# 1. Jesus Came to Give Us the Footsteps to Peace

> *"**To give light to them that sit in darkness** and in the shadow of death, **to guide our feet into the way of peace**."* (Luke 1:79)

Jesus came to give light to those that live in darkness. Without Christ, we live in the shadow of death. Jesus came to guide us out of that darkness and into His light. He knew that we were doomed to die separated from the Father, so He stepped into time and rescued all of humanity. He guides our feet into peace. He is a sure Guide who will never lead us astray.

> *"Now the God of hope **fill you with all joy and peace** in believing, **that ye may abound in hope**, through the power of the Holy Ghost."* (Romans 15:13)

Paul confirmed this idea here in Romans. He wrote that God is a God of joy and peace; and when we believe in Him, He brings us into joy and peace. We must believe to have this hope, and it is the Holy Ghost who empowers us to believe. Our hope will not fail because it is based in God. This hope is guaranteed to bring us peace.

# 2. We Have Peace with God by Redemption

If we want peace in our lives, we must first have peace with God. As mentioned before, we cannot have peace with ourselves, others, or the world around us without peace with God. The problem is sin. We cannot have peace with God while we are still in bondage to sin. Thankfully, God solved this problem by reconciling us to Himself through the redemption of Christ.

> *"Therefore being justified by faith, we have peace with God through our Lord Jesus Christ:*
>
> *By whom also we have access by faith into this grace wherein we stand, and rejoice in hope of the glory of God.*
>
> *And not only so, but we glory in tribulations also: knowing that tribulation worketh patience."* (Romans 5:1-3)

These verses are foundational to our understanding of redemption and peace with God. This verse is the starting point and core of the gospel. It explains the very beginning of the path to peace that God has provided in Christ. Peace comes from being justified by faith. When you put your faith in Jesus Christ, you begin walking the path to peace. Our faith is in the person and work of Christ. He lived the perfect life that we cannot; He died as the atonement for our sins, taking our sin upon Himself. He also rose from the dead, and guarantees our resurrection. He

## Peace comes from being justified by faith.

shall return again to demonstrate His power and victory over sin and death. These glorious truths reconcile us to God. We are no longer His enemy but have peace with Him. He forgives all our sin and makes us white as snow. We are no longer ruled by sin, but can live lives of peace pleasing to God. That is the wonderful result of Jesus' death and resurrection. We have passed from death to life.

We have access to the grace of God through faith. We do not earn God's grace through our good works. Faith alone can bring us into grace and peace. Paul says that we "stand firm" in this grace. This peace is so complete, and this grace is so powerful, that we glory even during times of trouble and persecution. How can we glory in tribulation? God promises to use tribulation to build patience in us, and patience is a virtue which we need greatly in our lives. Therefore, our peace is not dependent on our outward circumstances. Even when life is very difficult, we can abide in God's peace. We can handle any difficult person or event that comes into our life. We do not need to panic or worry because God has promised us His perfect peace, and we can rely on Him, no matter what.

## 3. We Must Not Be Casual about Having Peace

Peace is hugely important. If we do not appreciate that, we are in danger of neglecting it. We need peace both for our own well-being and for the well-being of all our relationships. We must pursue peace and value it. As I pointed out in chapter one, we must abide in God's peace and never become casual about it. Several passages warn us about becoming complacent about our peace, and they contain a consistent and simple theme throughout: We must avoid evil and seek peace.

> *"**Keep thy tongue from evil, and thy lips from speaking guile**.*
>
> *Depart from evil, and do good; **seek peace, and pursue it**."*          (Psalm 34:13-14)

Our tongues can get us into a lot of trouble. When we speak out of anger or bitterness, we hurt not only our own peace, but that of others too. This principle applies to more than the spoken word. The written word is just as powerful. Bitter and angry posts on social media can also keep us from abiding in peace. We must flee from evil words and deeds, and not allow them a foothold in our lives. Instead, we must actively pursue peace, walking in the footsteps of peace God has provided.

> *"**Flee also youthful lusts**: but **follow** righteousness, faith, charity, **peace**, with them that call on the Lord out of a pure heart.*
>
> *But **foolish and unlearned questions avoid**, knowing that they do gender strifes."*
> (2 Timothy 2:22-23)

In these verses Paul provides a contrast. He warns us to flee from youthful lusts in a way very similar to the psalm we just read. He also cautions us against unlearned questions, referring to petty speculations that can bring division and strife into our relationships. Then he tells us what we should pursue: righteousness, faith, love, and peace. Those who follow this path call on the Lord from a pure heart, which means their internal motives are pure. It should be noted, however, that growing in purity of heart is a process. When we first come to know the Lord, our motives are mixed. We are still dealing with our own agendas that are firmly embedded on our hard drive. As we practice following Jesus though, we discover our new creation and the gifts Jesus has placed within us. As time passes, our motives become more and more aligned with God's and our peace with Him deepens.

> *"And **the servant of the Lord must not strive; but be gentle** unto all men, apt to teach, patient."*     (2 Timothy 2:24)

Gentleness and peace are related. Those who walk in peace will exhibit gentle and patient behavior toward others. They will not strive impatiently. In this passage, Paul is describing the qualifications for office in the church, but this admonition is also true for all followers of Christ.

> *"For he that will love life, and see good days,* **let him refrain his tongue from evil, and his lips that they speak no guile.**
>
> *Let him eschew evil, and do good;* **let him seek peace, and ensue it**." (1 Peter 3:10-11)

We all want to live a happy life and see good days. Here Peter gives us the simple formula for that: We must not use evil or dishonest speech. How we choose to employ our tongues has great potential for evil or good. We will not have peace if we choose to use our tongues for evil or engage in falsehood. Instead, we must flee from evil, and choose the good. We must seek peace and *ensue* it. *Ensue* is another word for *pursue,* and it indicates that we must take an active role as we abide in peace. We must seek it with all our hearts. We cannot be casual in our pursuit of peace. Jesus has shown us the pathway to peace, but we must pursue it. We must choose to walk in it.

# 4. God's Peace Causes Us to Triumph

Christ has reconciled us to God through His work on the cross, therefore we have peace with God. That is our standing. The next step is to *receive* peace from God. When we abide in God's peace, we are victorious.

> *"These things I have spoken unto you, that* ***in me ye might have peace****. In the world ye shall have tribulation:* ***but be of good cheer; I have overcome the world.****"*
>                                                              (John 16:33)

In Romans 8:37, Paul reminded us that we are more than conquerors through Him that loved us. In this passage, John has recorded the similar words of Jesus. Jesus taught His disciples well, so they would be able to have peace in the world. He knew what they needed better than they did. As His followers, we not only have peace with God, but we also have peace in spite of living in this fallen world too. Jesus told them to be of good cheer because He had overcome the world. It does not matter what we face in our lives if we have His peace. We will face tough times, but we can face them knowing that we have the bountiful grace and peace of God. Being able to stand in peace and receive God's peace in any situation grants us the ability to stand firm in a way we could not before we knew Christ. We can rest in Him. Our strength is no longer our own, but His, and He is a Rock.

> *"****Now the Lord of peace himself give you peace always*** *by all means. The Lord be with you all."*          (2 Thessalonians 3:16)

This verse is a very encouraging component of the gospel of Christ. Paul is speaking a blessing on the church in Thessalonica and this blessing is for us as well. He says the Lord of peace Himself will give us peace. God is all-powerful and completely in control of peace. He is the One who promises to give us peace. This promise cannot fail. An important element of this promise is almost hidden in one little adverb: "always." God's peace does not come or go based on our circumstances. His is an abiding peace. Not only will He always give us peace, but He will do so by every possible means. Even though God's peace may come in different ways, we know He can be relied upon for it at all times. Our hearts and minds can rest in His peace because He is the Lord of peace who will always be faithful to us. His peace will never be taken away from us. This is good news.

# 5. More of God's Word Leads to More Peace

Let's turn our attention to the role that God's Word plays in our peace. Simply put, the more time we spend in God's Word, the more we will experience the peace of God.

> *"For my thoughts are not your thoughts, neither are your ways my ways, saith the LORD.*
>
> *For as the heavens are higher than the earth, **so are my ways higher than your ways, and my thoughts than your thoughts**.*"    (Isaiah 55:8-9)

God is different from man. (That should be obvious to everyone.) He is infinite while we are finite. He is perfect while we are sinful. He is omnipotent while we are very weak. The differences extend to our thoughts too. God's thoughts are perfect. He knows everything perfectly. Conversely, humanity's knowledge and thoughts are limited. God's ways are qualitatively different from man's ways too. His ways are perfect while ours are not.

Isaiah tells us that God's thoughts are infinitely greater than ours. To make his point clear, Isaiah uses an analogy: God's thoughts are higher than our thoughts just as the heavens are higher than the earth. Isaiah is not making a comparison between the ground and the clouds up in the sky. He is using the vastness of the universe to illustrate how much greater God's thoughts are than ours.

So how vast is this universe? Light travels at 186,000 miles per second. In one second, light can travel around the world 7½ times. There are more than thirty-one million seconds in a year. If you multiple thirty-one million times 186,000, you have the distance light travels in one year (or one light year). One light year is about six trillion miles. The closest galaxy to ours is *25,000* light years away, and scientists estimate that there are over 100 billion galaxies in the universe. These distances are unfathomable to our minds. This is the comparison Isaiah is making.      We cannot even conceive how much higher God's thoughts are than our own.

To put it another way, God is way smarter than we are. But here is the wonderful thing. God has chosen to reveal His thoughts to us in His Word, the Bible. We do not have to live in ignorance, but can think God's thoughts as we read His Word and hide it in our hearts. This is another mysterious process in which we exchange the worthless for the precious, and our inner man is strengthened and built up just by reading and listening to the written Word of God. Amazing!

> *"For as the rain cometh down, and the*
> *snow from heaven, and returneth not*

> *thither, but watereth the earth, and maketh*
> *it bring forth and bud, that it may give seed*
> *to the sower, and bread to the eater;*
>
> **So shall my word be that goeth forth out**
> **of my mouth: it shall not return unto me**
> **void, but it shall accomplish that which**
> **I please, and it shall prosper in the thing**
> **whereto I sent it.**
>
> *For ye shall go out with joy, and* **be led**
> **forth with peace***: the mountains and the*
> *hills shall break forth before you into*
> *singing, and all the trees of the field shall*
> *clap their hands.*
>
> *Instead of the thorn shall come up the fir*
> *tree, and instead of the brier shall come up*
> *the myrtle tree: and it shall be to the LORD*
> *for a name, for an everlasting sign that*
> *shall not be cut off."*      (Isaiah 55:10-13)

God's Word is powerful. It accomplishes what it sets out to do. The rain and snow do not just fall without watering the earth. Similarly, God's Word doesn't just come out of His mouth and not accomplish what He wants it to do. God created the universe by His Word. He spoke and everything came into existence out of nothing. God has given us His Word in the Bible, and it too is powerful. God wants His Word to transform our lives, bringing us peace and making us prosper.

When we appreciate and grow in God's Word, we will not only have peace, we will also have great joy. Isaiah used natural metaphors to describe this great joy: The mountains and hills will sing, and the tress will clap their hands. Instead of thorns and briers, creation will produce beautiful fir and myrtle trees. This imagery is one of delight so great that even the natural creation participates in it. This great joy is a sign to us that the peace God provides is everlasting and we shall never be cut off from it. This promise alone brings us great joy and happiness.

> *"But he answered and said, It is written,*
> **Man shall not live by bread alone**, *but by*
> *every word that proceedeth out of the mouth*
> *of God."*                    (Matthew 4:4)

Jesus clearly stated His point in this section, explaining that man cannot live on food alone. Although our "bread" may sustain our physical bodies, it is not enough to maintain our spiritual health. We must have the Word of God for our very survival. It is essential for our peace and well-being.

> *"Ye have heard that it hath been said, Thou*
> *shalt love thy neighbour, and hate thine*
> *enemy.*
>
> *But I say unto you,* **Love your enemies,**
> **bless them that curse you, do good to them**
> **that hate you, and pray for them which**
> **despitefully use you, and persecute you;**
>
> **That ye may be the children of your**
> **Father which is in heaven:** *for he maketh*
> *his sun to rise on the evil and on the good,*
> *and sendeth rain on the just and on the*
> *unjust."*                    (Matthew 5:43-45)

In this excerpt from the Sermon on the Mount, Jesus provided us with a radical Christian ethic. He instructed us to do things that make no sense to the world. The world advises us to take revenge on those who hurt us, but this choice does not lead to peace. The path to peace is through love and kindness—even for those who wrong us. Jesus taught us to bless them, do good to them, and pray for them instead. This makes perfect sense if we take the time to think about it. How can we have peace if we are cursing other people, or hating them, or plotting our revenge against them? The pathway to peace lies in gentleness and kindness towards those who are against us. If we follow these footsteps, we will abide in the peace of the Father as His children, and we will reflect the peace of our Father toward others at the same time.

> Jesus taught that withholding our forgiveness saps our peace.

> *"Then came Peter to him, and said, Lord, how oft shall my brother sin against me, and I forgive him? till seven times? Jesus saith unto him, I say not unto thee, until seven times: but, until **seventy times seven.**"* (Matthew 18:21-22)

Jesus taught that withholding our forgiveness saps our peace. Peter asked Him how often he should forgive somebody who sinned against him. Peter believed his suggestion of seven times was reasonable, even generous. Many of us have a difficult time forgiving somebody just once! Jesus, however, tells us to forgive our offenders 70 times 7. If you do the math, you will realize Jesus was telling Peter to forgive someone who wrongs him 490 times if he asked for forgiveness. God knows that holding a grudge prevents us from having peace, so Jesus taught that we should practice radical forgiveness. We must avoid bitterness and revenge and embrace forgiveness. We must cancel the debts of those who sin against us just as Jesus canceled the debt for our sin. This is the pathway to peace.

> *"And that ye **study to be quiet, and to do your own business**, and to work with your own hands, as we commanded you."*
> (1 Thessalonians 4:11)

Paul gave us frank and practical advice, directing that we mind our own business. We naturally stick our noses where they do not belong, and try to control other people and their actions. We will have so much more peace in our lives if we worry about our own problems instead of worrying about the problems of others. We do not need to manage all the problems in the world. The path to peace lies in minding one's own business.

# 6. Replace Worry with Prayer

Many people struggle with anxiety, panic, and worry. We tend to sweat the small stuff—in addition to the urgent. We want to have control over our lives, but often feel like life is out of our control. God has a simple prescription for anxiety: prayer.

> *"Be careful for nothing; but **in every thing by prayer and supplication with thanksgiving let your requests be made known unto God.**
>
> **And the peace of God**, which passeth all understanding, shall keep your hearts and minds through Christ Jesus."*
> (Philippians 4:6-7)

This passage is so vital to understanding God's peace that we will necessarily look at it over and over again. Paul wrote that we should be careful for nothing. This means we should not be anxious about our situation in life. We should not be worried about our circumstances. Instead of worrying, we should pray. When we make our requests known to God with thanksgiving, He will give us His peace. This does not mean that everything will be easy, but it does mean we can have genuine peace in every circumstances because we have placed our burdens on the Lord. God assures us that He loves us and cares for us; therefore, we can have peace and rest. Eugene H. Peterson's paraphrase of this passage in *The Message* provides a helpful reflection. He renders it thus,

> *"Don't fret or worry.* **Instead of worrying, pray. Let petitions and praises shape your worries into prayers, letting God know your concerns.**
>
> *Before you know it, a sense of God's wholeness, everything coming together for good, will come and settle you down. It's wonderful what happens when Christ displaces worry at the center of your life."*
> (Philippians 4:6-7 MSG)

Prayer is absolutely necessary to our growth in the Lord. Consider it this way: When you get married, your life changes deeply. Now instead of being alone, you wake up next to your husband or wife. Instead of coming home from work to an empty home, there is another human being there too. That other person is now actively involved in every decision you will ever make—from which restaurant you will visit together to what house you will buy and where you will live. This companion shares your deepest fears and worst failures as well as your happiest experiences and most joyful and intimate moments. And what is one of the hallmarks of this successful relationship? Honest communication. Without it, that marriage will fail.

Without prayer, our relationship with Jesus never can be what it should either, but through prayer, we share everything with Christ and gain His help in it. E. M. Bounds wrote this:

> The ministry of prayer has been the peculiar distinction of all of God's saints. This has been the secret of their power. The energy and the soul of their work has been the closet. The need of help outside of man being so great, man's natural inability to always judge kindly, justly, and truly, and to act the Golden Rule, so prayer is enjoined by Christ to enable man to act in all these things according to the divine will. By prayer, the ability is secured to feel the law of love, to speak according to the law of love, and to do everything in harmony with the law of love.[8]

We need God every day. To walk in His peace, we must pray.

# 7. Following God's Wisdom Always Brings Peace

*"I will hear what God the Lord will speak:*
*for **he will speak peace** unto his people, and*

---

8       E. M. Bounds, *The Complete Works of E. M. Bounds on Prayer* (Grand Rapids, Michigan: Baker Books, 1980), 151.

> to his saints: **but let them not turn again to
> folly.**"                               (Psalm 85:8)

Proverbs teaches us that folly is the opposite of wisdom, and this psalm warns against turning to folly. When we do not listen to the Word of God, we will fall into folly. The path of folly does not lead to peace. Folly brings trials and tribulation. If we want the Lord's peace, we must follow the path of wisdom found in His Word.

> *"Those things, which ye have both learned,
> and received, and heard, and seen in me,*
> ***do: and the God of peace shall be with
> you.***"                               (Philippians 4:9)

We often confuse wisdom with intelligence. We think that if someone has great intellectual abilities, they also have wisdom, but there is a huge difference between being smart and being wise. Proverbs 9:10 tells us that the fear of the Lord is the beginning of wisdom. The fear of the Lord implies a respect for God that leads to a life of obedience submitted to His Lordship and authority. Paul reminds us that when we learn from God's Word and obey it, God will bring us peace.

> *"But if ye have bitter envying and strife in
> your hearts, glory not, and lie not against
> the truth.*
>
> *This wisdom descendeth not from above,
> but is earthly, sensual, devilish.*
>
> *For where envying and strife is, there is
> confusion and every evil work.*

> **But the wisdom that is from above is first**
> **pure, then peaceable,** *gentle, and easy to*
> *be intreated, full of mercy and good fruits,*
> *without partiality, and without hypocrisy.*
>
> *And the fruit of righteousness is sown in*
> *peace of them that make peace."*
>
> (James 3:14-18)

James provides excellent teaching on peace in this passage. I have kept these verses together because the argument flows together. First, James describes the absence of peace. Where peace is absent, there is envy, strife, confusion, bitterness, and evil. If there is a lack of God's presence, there is no peace.

Next, James turns to a description of wisdom. Wisdom is peaceable, pure, and gentle. Good works flow out of peace, while evil works flow out of chaos or the absence of peace. Wisdom and peace are not partial or filled with hypocrisy. If they come from God, they are genuine. Peace only flows from the presence of God.

# 8. Keep in Step with the Holy Spirit

Right before Jesus ascended to the right hand of the Father, He promised that He would send the Holy Spirit to be with His people. This promise was fulfilled in Acts 2 at Pentecost. The Holy Spirit has not left, but still comes alongside His people as a Comforter. He is called the *paraclete* which means Helper and Advocate. He helps us into the path of peace and keeps us in it.

> *"But the fruit of the Spirit is love, joy,*
> **peace,** *longsuffering, gentleness, goodness,*
> *faith,*

> *Meekness, temperance: against such there*
> *is no law.*"        (Galatians 5:22-23)

Most of us remember the "fruit of the spirit" found in Galatians. We tend to rattle off that fruit list without reflecting on what it means. However, it is important to remember that peace is part of the fruit listed by Paul. When the Holy Spirit indwells us, we have peace. The fruit all hang together. When we have peace, we will have the other fruit too.

> *"With all lowliness and meekness, with*
> *longsuffering, forbearing one another in*
> *love;*
>
> *endeavouring to keep the unity of the Spirit*
> **in the bond of peace.**"        (Ephesians 4:2-3)

Scripture uses the imagery of a dove to describe the Holy Spirit. The dove also symbolizes peace. This is not an accident. If we keep in lockstep with the Spirit and are bound to Him, we will maintain the bond of peace. How do we do this? We must be lowly and meek. We must love one another and be patient with one another. We must be quick to forgive and never hold grudges. We must live at peace with one another. Just as we are united to Christ through the Holy Spirit, we are united to one another in Christ. We must keep the unity of these bonds in peace.

# 9. Stay at Peace with Everyone

We cannot be at peace with some people and enemies with others. Even though it is easier to live peaceably with some people than with others, we must remain at peace with *all* people inasmuch as it depends upon us. We are going to look at several verses in Romans that teach this principle.

> *"Recompense to **no man evil for evil.***
> *Provide things honest in the sight of **all***
> *men.*
>
> *If it be possible**, as much as lieth in you,***
> ***live peaceably with all men.***
>
> *Dearly beloved, **avenge not yourselves,***
> *but rather give place unto wrath: for it is*
> *written, Vengeance is mine; I will repay,*
> *saith the Lord.*
>
> *Therefore, if thine enemy hunger, feed him;*
> *if he thirst, give him drink: for in so doing*
> *thou shalt heap coals of fire on his head.*
>
> *Be not overcome of evil but overcome **evil***
> ***with good.** "* (Romans 12:17-21)

If somebody wrongs us, we instinctively want to repay that wrong in kind. That's how revenge works. This is our natural, sinful tendency. Paul urges just the opposite. He tells us never to return evil for evil, but provide honest things in the sight of all men instead. If men are evil toward us, we must not be evil toward them. If they are obnoxious or falsely accuse us or wrong us in any way, we must not return their evil with evil. Choosing to not do this helps us remain at peace with all men and keeps us in the pathway to God's peace.

We are able to do this because we know that we are God's "dearly beloved"; we don't have to worry about defending ourselves. God will watch after our interests. Vengeance and recompense are the business of our Lord, not us. He will look after ultimate justice against those who wrong us, and make equitable choices for us. We can rest in peace, knowing that God's justice is perfect in both its scope and timing. However, sometimes it seems that God does not take justice on our enemies when they wrong us. Why is this? We must remember that if we take justice into our own hands, God will step back and not provide justice in His way. Also, we must remember that God provides ultimate justice in His own timing. Too often we are impatient with the justice of God and want to take things into our own hands.

Instead of seeking revenge, what should we do? We should shower our enemy with undeserved kindness. If he is hungry, we should buy him a burger. If he is thirsty, we should get him a Coke…or better yet a Pellegrino. If we treat our enemy this way, Paul says we will heap burning coals on his head. At first glance this might look like we are doing something cruel to our enemies. After all, nobody wants to have a burning hot coal on their bare scalp! However, Paul was referring to an act of kindness.

In Roman times, if a person went on a long journey in cold weather, they carried hot coals in a blanket on their head. Then when it came time to rest on the side of the road, they had a toasty blanket to keep them warm. We are to be a blessing and comfort to our enemies by showering them with kindness, even when they are cruel. We leave vengeance to the Lord. In this way, we will not be overcome with evil, but overcome evil with good.

# 10. Peace Is Our Mission in Life

If we have peace with God, then we can have peace with others and peace *in every circumstance*. Genuine peace is fundamental to our well-being and a great blessing to those around us. We are going to examine several passages that teach this principle.

> *"Blessed are the peacemakers: for **they***
> ***shall be called the children of God.***"
> (Matthew 5:9)

This simple passage from the Beatitudes is a great comfort. The greatest blessing in the world is to be called a child of God. Jesus tells us that peacemaking is central to our lives because it brings this blessing. We must carry the message of peace to others. What a privilege being a peacemaker is!

> *"How beautiful upon the mountains are*
> *the feet **of him that bringeth good tidings,***
> ***that publisheth peace;** that bringeth good*
> *tidings of good, that publisheth salvation;*
> *that saith unto Zion, Thy God reigneth!"*
> (Isaiah 52:7)

This verse is repeated in the New Testament, but we want to look at it first in the Old Testament. In ancient Israel, messages were conveyed by foot. They did not have Internet, radio, telegrams, or even the pony express. Messengers ran barefoot from place to place to spread important news. If the news they brought was good, news of peace and prosperity, the people rejoiced that the messenger came.

Their feet would be considered "beautiful" even though their outward appearance might be rough. The feet of messengers were commonly broken, cut, and bruised because they traveled over mountain footpaths, but they were spreading the message of peace and salvation. This good news that God reigns is beautiful, so the feet of those who carry this news are beautiful too. God wants us to carry on this task of spreading peace and good news to the world.

> *"And how shall they preach, except they be sent? as it is written,* **How beautiful are the feet of them that preach the gospel of peace**, *and bring glad tidings of good things!"*     (Romans 10:15)

Paul alludes to that same passage from Isaiah in Romans. Not everyone is called to enter full-time gospel ministry, but *we are all called to participate in this ministry*. We can send and support those who preach the good news of peace to the world. We should also be prepared to share the good news with others as opportunities present themselves. This is our mission as the body of believers.

> *"Be not deceived; God is not mocked: for* **whatsoever a man soweth**, *that* **shall he also reap**.*"*     (Galatians 6:7)

We reap what we sow. If you plant tomato seeds, you should not expect to pull carrots out of the ground. Similarly, if you sow hatred and dissent, you should not expect to reap peace. If our mission is not bringing peace to others as God intends, how can we expect to enjoy God's blessing of genuine peace?

> **"Give, and it shall be given unto you; good measure, pressed down, and shaken together, and running over, shall men give into your bosom.** *For with the same*

> *measure that ye mete withal it* **shall be**
> **measured to you** *again."* (Luke 6:38)

Jesus makes this principle very clear in the gospel of Luke. When we are generous with peace and kindness, we will receive peace and kindness. We do not run out of peace when we share it with others. In fact, the opposite happens. The more peace we give to others, the more peace we will experience in our lives. When we are a blessing to others, we will find that we receive more in return than we gave. If you give away your life, you will find your life given back, but not merely given back—given back with bonus and blessing. Generosity begets generosity, and this is especially true of peace.

> *"And* **let the peace of God rule in your**
> **hearts**, *to the which also ye are called in*
> *one body; and be ye thankful."*
> (Colossians 3:15)

# Summing Up

We have learned more about the pathway to peace. God not only provides His peace, but teaches us the steps we must take to attain it. First, we let the peace of God rule in our hearts. We give Jesus control of our lives, and He reconciles us to God, so that we have peace with Him. We abide in this peace by abiding in the Word of God, following His wisdom instead of our own. Then we can spread peace to others by becoming a blessing to them, even when they wrong us. These are the pathways to genuine peace. Let us be thankful for them. God's powerful peace reaches into every relationship and circumstance. Truly in Him, we overcome the world.

# Chapter 4

# The Power of Genuine Peace

In the first chapter, we learned that the world's peace is dependent on feelings and circumstances, while God's peace is completely independent of all that. What a difference! God's peace helps us remain calm in the face of turmoil because it affects the inward condition of our heart and mind. Those trying to attain the world's peace are doomed to a futile existence focused on trying to control the external happenings of their lives. Since we control virtually nothing, this is a fruitless and worthless task.

We further defined genuine peace as a "realm where chaos is not permitted to enter." In chapters two and three, we learned about God's path to peace, and in this chapter, we will be examining another important difference between the world's peace and God's peace: its power. God's peace cannot be destroyed or usurped, while the world's peace is transitory and dying. It does not have the power of God's peace.

*"Peace I leave with you, my peace I give unto you: **not as the world giveth, give I***

> ***unto you***. *Let not your heart be troubled,*
> *neither let it be afraid."*          (John 14:27)

Jesus said that when we have His peace, our hearts will not be troubled, and we will not be afraid. He told His disciples this fact right before He went to the cross, a time when He knew their faith would be tested and they would be afraid. Jesus purposefully left them a peace that was not like the world's peace. The peace of Jesus provides a chaos-free zone. Our outward circumstances—no matter how terrible—cannot remove Jesus' peace from our hearts.

## The peace of Jesus provides a chaos-free zone.

Jesus' peace grants us a quietness and serenity of heart, enabling us to "hold our peace" even in the most trying circumstances. We can refrain from criticism and complaining when people wrong us or when life does not go our way. We can be reconciled with others. Peace unifies us with our fellow man and keeps us from strife. We can be calm and composed. We can have order in our life instead of disorder. We can have feelings of love, empathy, and kindness, instead of hostility and discord. Genuine peace brings with it the power of lasting reconciliation. Jesus' peace has the power to change the world one relationship at a time.

> *"But the wicked are like the troubled sea,*
> *when it cannot rest, whose waters cast up*
> *mire and dirt.*
>
> ***There is no peace***, *saith my God*, ***to the***
> ***wicked.***"                    (Isaiah 57:20-21)

84

Isaiah provides a contrast with genuine peace in this verse. The imagery is powerful. Few things are as troubled and chaotic as a storm at sea. Waves can toss ships about as if they were twigs. When a powerful hurricane sweeps ashore, it flattens houses and uproots trees. This is the picture Isaiah used to describe the wicked man's state of mind. He can have no peace. His life is continually driven by anxiety, fear, and worry.

# 1. Peace Holds the Power of Freedom from Internal Bondage

*"If the Son therefore shall make you free, ye shall be free indeed."*      (John 8:36)

This freedom comes from God's peace within us. Eugene Peterson wrote this:

*Shalom,* "peace," is one of the richest words in the Bible. You can no more define it by looking in the dictionary than you can define a person by his or her social security number. It gathers all aspects of wholeness that result from God's will being completed in us. It is the work of God that, when complete, releases streams of living water in us and pulsates with eternal life. Every time Jesus healed, forgave or called someone, we have a demonstration of *shalom.*[9]

That's the peace Jesus exhibited and the peace we can access through Him. It frees us like nothing else ever could.

---

9      Eugene Peterson, *A Long Obedience in the Same Direction: Discipleship in an Instant Society* (Downers Grove, IL: InterVarsity Press, 1980).

Jesus Christ freed us through the work of the cross. He gives us internal freedom from the bondage of anxiety, tension, panic, stress, confusion, and fear. True freedom is not the ability to do whatever we want to do. Doing whatever we want is *license*, not freedom. Freedom is the ability to rest in the peace and assurance of God. It is the freedom to do what is right. We are no longer slaves to sinful bondage when we turn control of our life over to Christ. Freedom in Christ brings emotional well-being. License brings heartache and disturbance. God's peace can pour through us just as it did Jesus.

> *"For God hath not given us the spirit of fear; **but of power, and of love, and of a sound mind.**"* (2 Timothy 1:7)

Fear comes from the world, not God. God has given us power, love, and a sound mind. These three things are all components of genuine peace. Peace is the foundation of good mental health, while fear produces bondage.

Our emotions should not be our masters. Instead, they should serve us. We need them, but they should not be in the driver's seat. If they are, they will lead us astray from the path of peace. Our emotions have a purpose. They should provide the energy we need to make wise choices. Without them, we would be paralyzed by apathy. Even though our emotions spark our actions, they should not be our guidance system. The wisdom of God should be our guidance system while our emotions provide the energy to move us in the right direction. Our emotions must never interfere with our wisdom, but be submitted to God.[10]

---

10    For more helpful information about controlling our emotions, see the videos, "How to Control Your Emotions," "How to Properly Control Your Emotions," "Truth, Life, and Emotions," and "How to Control Your Imaginations" at our website https://nothingbutthetruth.org.

## 2. Peace Provides the Power of Freedom from Outside Disturbances

*"Behold, **I give unto you power to tread on serpents and scorpions, and over all the power of the enemy**: and nothing shall by any means hurt you."* (Luke 10:19)

Peace is not limited to protecting us from inner bondage. Christ's peace protects us from external attacks from the Enemy as well. The Devil's forces want to take away our peace, but they are helpless against the power of the Lord. Nothing shall be able by any means to damage the peace that we have with the Lord. Even when we feel weak, He will fight for us and restore our peace.

> **Freedom is the ability to rest in the peace and assurance of God.**

*"Who art thou that judgest another man's servant? to his own master he standeth or falleth. Yea, he shall be holden up: for **God is able to make him stand**."*
(Romans 14:4)

We belong to God. He holds us up and makes us stand. We need not fear any outside source because no outside force can take away our peace. We do not need to be intimidated by anyone or anything either. We do not need to worry about the opinions of the world or become prisoners of another's expectations. We are not ruled by anger, vengeance, strife, chaos, or faulty judgment. We are not controlled by the forces of this world. Instead, we can live in peace, resting on the promises of God. This state is a powerful part of our inheritance in Christ.

# 3. Peace Gives Us the Power of Emotional Stability and Self-control

God's peace produces emotional stability and self-control.[11] When we have inner peace in our hearts and minds, we are not governed by wildly swinging emotions. Instead, we can control them and let them be guided by the wisdom of God. They are held in check and we are protected, but this depends on our choice to trust God instead of allowing our emotions to rule us.

> *"That **we henceforth be no more children, tossed to and fro**, and carried about with every wind of doctrine, by the sleight of men, and cunning craftiness, whereby they lie in wait to deceive."*       (Ephesians 4:14)

When we lack self-control, we are susceptible to the lies of wicked and deceitful men. They can lead us astray with false doctrine. Paul warns us against a lack of self-control and being carried away by cunning men. When we stay in the path of peace, we will not be easily manipulated by others.

> *"And now, behold, I go bound in the spirit unto Jerusalem, not knowing the things that shall befall me there:*

---

11        For further teaching on self-control, visit our website https:// nothingbutthetruth.org, and view the video, "How to Develop Emotional Intelligence."

> *Save that the Holy Ghost witnesseth in every city, saying that bonds and afflictions abide me.*
>
> *But **none of these things move me**, neither count I my life dear unto myself, so that I might finish my course with joy, and the ministry, which I have received of the Lord Jesus, to testify the gospel of the grace of God."* (Acts 20:22-24)

We do not need to know what the future holds to have peace. Paul knew that the gospel of Christ would spread and triumph. This was enough to give him peace as he went in chains to Rome. He knew that he would have peace and joy in jail and in death. His hope did not depend on his outward circumstances, but on the gospel of grace. This was the same Paul who had once persecuted Christians and sought the destruction of the church as a zealous Jew. This former persecutor was so transformed by the gospel of peace that he was able to face his own persecution for the cause of Christ with serenity and joy. He had the peace that passes understanding, and God wants us to experience the blessings of that same peace. Let's look at the practical outworking of this process.

# 4. Peace Gives Us the Power to Control Our Speech

> *"**Death and life are in the power of the tongue:** and they that love it shall eat the fruit thereof."* (Proverbs 18:21)

Our words can be a blessing to ourselves and others—or they can be a curse. Our speech, like every aspect of our lives, needs to be submitted to the power of God's peace. We are going to look at several more passages which explain the importance of speech for our peace and our relationships with God and others.

> *"How forcible are right words!* ***but what doth your arguing reprove?"*** (Job 6:25)

In this verse, Job is answering one of his "comforters." Job was put to the test when the Lord allowed Satan to bring calamities into his life. Instead of speaking words of comfort to a righteous man who was suffering, Job's friends condemned him, saying that the horrible things that had happened to him were caused by his sin. Job pointed out that while his friends might be using forceful words, their arguments were worthless. Arguments and accusations do not accomplish anything. They disturb our peace and the peace of those around us. When we focus on winning an argument, we are defending our own egos instead of serving our brothers and sisters. When our speech is controlled by peace, we will speak words of peace and comfort to those who are suffering.

> ***"A soft answer turneth away wrath****: but grievous words stir up anger.*
>
> ***The tongue of the wise useth knowledge aright****: but the mouth of fools poureth out foolishness."* (Proverbs 15:1-2)

Proverbs confirms what we learned in Job. In this passage we learn that a soft answer turns away anger. We might win the argument, but we really accomplish nothing with harsh words. Gentle words are wise words. Combative words are foolish ones. Most of the time when words cause conflict, the cause of the disagreement does not lie with the words or opinions themselves, *but in the way that they are presented.* Harsh words lead to an escalation of feeling instead of rational discourse. This passage teaches that our words should not just be gentle and peaceful, but also wholesome and good. Foul language does not bring peace.

> *"Righteous lips are the delight of kings;*
> *and they love him that speaketh right."*
> (Proverbs 16:13)

Our words should not only be kind and gentle, they must also be wholesome and righteous. Coarse language does not bring peace, nor do evil words and lies. Righteousness and truth, however, bring delight.

> *"She openeth her mouth with wisdom;*
> *and in her tongue is the law of kindness."*
> (Proverbs 31:26)

Proverbs 31 famously describes the virtuous woman. The woman of virtue is valued and sought after. One of her most important features is her use of words. She speaks with wisdom and kindness. Her speech is controlled by the power of God's peace so that she is a blessing to those around her.

> *"The Lord GOD hath given me the tongue*
> *of the learned, **that I should know how***
> ***to speak a word in season to him that is***
> ***weary:** he wakeneth morning by morning,*
> *he wakeneth mine ear to hear as the*
> *learned."* (Isaiah 50:4)

In this passage, the prophet Isaiah reminds us of the importance of thinking before we speak. Too often our tendency is to say whatever rash thought pops into our heads. Isaiah urges us to use *learned* speech: speech infused with the wisdom of peace. This means we should think before we speak. We should respond and not react. If we do not heed this advice, we will live to regret it. Learned words bring help, healing, comfort, and peace to others.

> *"O generation of vipers,* **how can ye,**
> **being evil, speak good things?** *for out*
> *of the abundance of the heart the mouth*
> *speaketh."*                    (Matthew 12:34)

> **We should boldly proclaim the truth of the gospel in a gentle and calm way.**

Jesus described what happens when people fail to follow the instruction of Isaiah. Since words come from the heart, they indicate the condition of our hearts. When the heart is evil, the words that come pouring out of the mouth are evil too. The tongue reflects what is going on within us. If our heart is controlled by peace, our words will convey this peace.

> *"But* **speaking the truth in love, may grow**
> **up into him in all things**, *which is the head,*
> *even Christ."*                    (Ephesians 4:15)

Peace does not gloss over the truth. It speaks the truth in love. People may not like the message of the gospel, but we are called to proclaim it in love. We can do this because of the power of peace over our speech. We should boldly proclaim the truth of the gospel in a gentle and calm way.

> *"And **the tongue is a fire, a world of iniquity**: so is the tongue among our members, that **it defileth the whole body, and setteth on fire the course of nature; and it is set on fire of hell.***
>
> *For every kind of beasts, and of birds, and of serpents, and of things in the sea, is tamed, and hath been tamed of mankind:*
>
> ***But the tongue can no man tame**; it is an unruly evil, full of deadly poison."*
>
> (James 3:6-8)

James warns of the power of the tongue to do evil. When our tongues lack the controlling power of God's speech, they defile our whole bodies. Our tongues can harm us and others too. They are as powerful as a raging fire; and when controlled and directed by our own egos, they are full of danger.

> *"Speak not evil one of another, brethren.* ***He that speaketh evil of his brother, and judgeth his brother, speaketh evil of the law, and judgeth the law***: but if thou judge the law, thou art not a doer of the law, but a judge."* (James 4:11)

God commands us not to speak evil of our brothers. This is a violation of His law. When we do this, we set ourselves above God's law as if we could judge it. Instead our words should be controlled by the power of peace. When our words are controlled by peace, they will be a blessing to everyone, including ourselves. When they are controlled by our own whims, they are a danger and curse instead.

## 5. Peace Gives Us the Power to Speak Like God

Conversely, we can speak God's words after Him. As we receive it, we can speak God's truth with power, love, and conviction. Before we look at some verses which explain what this means, we will look at some verses that give us a contrast to it.

> *"Talk no more so exceeding proudly;* **let not arrogancy come out of your mouth:** *for the LORD is a God of knowledge, and by him actions are weighed."* (1 Samuel 2:3)

God tells us not to speak arrogantly. God, who has all knowledge, must rule our speech. He weighs all our actions—including our speech. He does not tolerate proud speech which seeks to usurp Him. He will bring down the proud, but lift and bless those who are humble.

> *"**Will ye speak wickedly for God?** and talk deceitfully for him?"* (Job 13:7)

Once again, Job is responding to his false friends. These presumptuous friends had the gall to speak false words *as if they were speaking for God.* They accused Job of sin that he had not committed. Whenever we slander another person, we are not speaking like God with the power of peace. Job called them out by asking them this rhetorical question: "Will ye speak wickedly for God?"

Job knew God's peace internally, so he could recognize the evil behind their charges. Job knew God loved and cared for him.

> *"That **thou turnest thy spirit against***
> ***God**, and lettest such words go out of thy*
> *mouth?"*                    (Job 15:13)

These words came from the mouth of Eliphaz, one of Job's accusers. After Job's speech, he continued slandering Job. You can see how his harsh words did not bring peace. Eliphaz abandoned the power of God's peaceful speech in his words.

> *"And **thou shalt speak unto him, and put***
> ***words in his mouth**: and I will be with thy*
> *mouth, and with his mouth, and will teach*
> *you what ye shall do."*          (Exodus 4:15)

This verse describes how speech *should* operate in our lives. Moses did not want to speak on God's behalf, but God reassured him by telling him that he could speak through Aaron. God gave Moses the words to give to Aaron, so that God's words could be spoken to Pharaoh and the Israelites. There are many instances of this kind of promise to the prophets. God was assuring them that He would speak faithful and true words that were from Him.

> *"The preparations of the heart in man,*
> ***and the answer of the tongue, is from the***
> ***LORD**."*                  (Proverbs 16:1)

God has prepared our hearts to speak His words after Him too. This process is amply explained throughout the

Bible. God desires that we live in peace with others in our lives. The fruit of the joy and love He gives us in our hearts is the gift of peaceful speech. This is only found in the Lord.

> **"Let your speech be always with grace,**
> **seasoned with salt**, *that ye may know how*
> *ye ought to answer every man."*
>
> (Colossians 4:6)

God's grace should season our speech, just as salt seasons our food. When our speech is seasoned with grace (salt), we will know how to answer every person as God desires. Since God has shown us grace, we can reflect that same grace to others in our speech. When we do this, we are speaking like God. It is peace that gives us the power to do this, and it is an incredible blessing to us as well as them.

> *"If any man speak,* **let him speak as the**
> **oracles of God**; *if any man minister, let him*
> *do it as of the ability which God giveth:*
> **that God in all things may be glorified**
> **through Jesus Christ**, *to whom be praise*
> *and dominion for ever and ever. Amen."*
>
> (1 Peter 4:11)

Since peaceful speech has the power to allow us to speak God's words, we should speak to others the same way that God has spoken. We should speak the truth in love as God has done in His Word. We should speak as though God were speaking through us *all the time*. One easy way of doing this is to speak Scripture to one another. We do not have to guess what God would say about many things because He has spoken to us clearly in His Word. It is difficult to be angry with another person when you speak truthful words in a loving way. It is even more difficult to be angry with somebody when speaking Scripture. When we speak in this way, we glorify God through Jesus Christ, and live in harmony with others.

# 6. Peace Gives Us the Power of Quiet

> *"**In the multitude of words there wanteth not sin**: but he that refraineth his lips is wise."* (Proverbs 10:19)

Have you ever noticed that people who are anxious tend to talk a lot? The opposite is also true. People who are peaceful tend to use fewer words. They are not trying to fill empty moments, but are content to listen. When we speak out of anxiety, we also tend to say the wrong thing. Our insecurity leads us into trouble. Unchecked, too many words can produce wrong attitudes and behaviors down the road.

> *"**He that hath knowledge spareth his words**: and a man of understanding is of an excellent spirit.*
>
> *Even a fool, when he holdeth his peace, is counted wise: and he that shutteth his lips is esteemed a man of understanding."* (Proverbs 17:27-28)

You may have heard the saying, "Better to remain silent and appear to be a fool than to open your mouth and remove all doubt." This proverb was probably the source for that quote. It teaches us that foolishness is revealed only when that person starts talking. A fool's outward appearance may be impressive; but when he speaks, his foolish heart is made known. A person with true knowledge and peace will remain quiet until the proper time.

> *"**Speak not in the ears of a fool***: *for he will despise the wisdom of thy words."*
> (Proverbs 23:9)

If you have ever argued with a person who refuses to listen to reasonable arguments, you know the truth of this proverb. We should not waste wise words on foolish people whose hearts are hardened and refuse to listen to the wisdom of God's peace. Speaking wise words to foolish people is a waste of time. As Jesus said in Matthew:

> *"**Give not that which is holy unto the dogs***, *neither cast ye your pearls before swine, lest they trample them under their feet, and turn again and rend you."* (Matthew 7:6)

> *"**Seest thou a man that is hasty in his words?*** *there is more hope of a fool than of him."* (Proverbs 29:20)

If we do not have the peace of God, we are likely to speak before we think. Those who talk without thinking often regret their words, and end up putting themselves in difficult situations. They needlessly offend others. When we have peace, we realize that we can calm ourselves before we respond in a conversation. We can think about our words and stay on the path to peace. It's impossible to take back our words or control their consequences once we say them—or even worse, print them. This story illustrates the problem well:

> In the washroom of a place of business in London, British newspaper publisher William Beaverbrook happened to meet Edward Heath, a young member of Parliament, about whom Beaverbrook had printed an insulting article a few days earlier. "My dear chap," said the publisher, embarrassed by the meeting, "I've been thinking it over, and I was wrong. Here and now, I wish to apologize."
>
> "Very well," grunted Heath, "but the next time, I wish you'd insult me in the washroom and apologize in your newspaper."[12]

> *"The words of wise men are heard in quiet more than **the cry of him that ruleth among fools**."*     (Ecclesiastes 9:17)

People believe that they need to say outrageous things to get attention. Social media rewards hyperbole, sarcasm, and outrage, but Ecclesiastes reminds us that this is an unwise choice. A quick word might seem appropriate, even witty, in the eyes of the world, but our words have more force and influence when they are spoken quietly and with wisdom.

> *"The beginning of the words of his mouth is foolishness: and the end of his talk is **mischievous madness**."*
>
> (Ecclesiastes 10:13)

---

12     Clifton Fadiman, "You Can't Take It Back," from the *The Little Brown Book of Anecdotes*, Ministry127, accessed June 3, 2021, https://ministry127.com/resources/illustration/you-can-t-take-it-back.

The words of a fool are not governed by the wisdom of God so they do not produce peace. They are mischievous and do not accomplish anything good. Instead, they bring trouble. Fools multiply their words to no purpose. We should not utter foolish words or listen to them.

> *"Of these things put them in remembrance, charging them before the Lord that **they strive not about words to no profit**, but to the subverting of the hearers.*
>
> *Study to shew thyself approved unto God, a workman that needeth not to be ashamed, rightly dividing the word of truth.*
>
> *But **shun profane and vain babblings**: for they will increase unto more ungodliness."*
> (2 Timothy 2:14-16)

Paul warns Timothy against pointless speech in this passage. Have you ever met someone who seems to talk just to hear their own voice? Their words have no value, but in fact, cause harm to others. Instead, we should listen to God's Word. Profane words and useless words do not lead us into God's path of peace, but subvert it instead.

> *"**But foolish and unlearned questions avoid, knowing that they do gender strifes**.*
>
> *And the servant of the Lord must not strive; but be gentle unto all men, apt to teach, patient,*
>
> *In meekness instructing those that oppose themselves; if God peradventure will give them repentance to the acknowledging of the truth."* (2 Timothy 2:23-25)

Foolish words and speculation lead to strife and division, causing people to waste time arguing over things that are unimportant. We destroy our own peace and the peace of others when we engage in this kind of behavior. Instead we should work to maintain true peace. There are great benefits when we do. Jon Huckins and Jer Swigart commented on their experience in helping a group of leaders with this in their book, *Mending the Divides: Creative Love in a Conflicted World.* They wrote:

> Recently we found ourselves around a table with a team of…leaders from an influential Midwestern church. Their restlessness was palpable. "Peace has been one of our core values for years," they said, "but our community is saturated with conflict. It's pervasive! Will you help us?" When we asked them to describe the implications of their dilemma, they spoke of a conflict-saturated staff culture, the inability to experience healthy disagreement among leaders and volunteers, the uptick of marriages and families within the church dissolving, and an inability to collaborate with other local churches to address local issues.
>
> The leaders went on to express their sense of helplessness as they watched issues of racism and injustice surge in their neighborhoods and armed conflicts accelerate around the world…At last, they disclosed just how far their church was from the reality of peace: "We're experts at identifying, discussing, and gossiping about conflict, but ultimately, we choose to either ignore it, run away from it, or engage it violently." As we dug in with this team, we asked them to consider how they were contributing to the conflicts in the church.

It was a risky question to ask a bunch of leaders who had spent more time diagnosing the problem then examining their own motives, intentions, and behavior...By meal's end, they had begun the hard work of acknowledging how their pride and pursuit of power had created a culture of conflict in the congregation. They realized that if they wanted to become an embodiment of peace in their city, they first needed to confront their own pride, repent of it, and begin moving through rather than around the conflicts that existed within the family.[13]

If we are to be peacemakers, we must deal with our own hearts in the process first. We need to see how we contribute to conflict around us, repent, and choose the path of God's peace. When we have real peace in our own hearts, then we can minister His peace to those around us.

The way of peace lies in gentle, meek, and patient words. We must speak the truth to people with kindness and love, not wrangle with them about inconsequential issues. Gracious speech, full of truth and mercy, will lead unbelievers into repentance and true faith. We should quietly admonish those who need correction with as few words as possible, and be authentic models ourselves.

# 7. Peace Gives Us the Power to Speak Acceptably to God

When we have God's peace, we can speak in a way that is pleasing and acceptable to God. We can speak acceptable words *about* Him—and *to* Him. When we have

---

13      Jon Huckins & Jer Swigart, *Mending the Divides: Creative Love in a Conflicted World* (Downers Grove, Illinois: IVP Books, 2017).

peace with Him, we can offer Him acceptable offerings of praise. When we do this, our peace grows even stronger.

> *"Let the words of my mouth, and the meditation of my heart, **be acceptable in thy sight, O LORD**, my strength, and my redeemer."* (Psalm 19:14)

Our external and internal words should be acceptable to God; that's the goal. They go hand-in-hand because our speech reflects the condition of our heart. When our heart is governed by God's peace, our thoughts and words are acceptable before God too. Before we say anything, we should always take a moment to reflect on what we are about to say and be sure our words are flowing from a peaceful heart. We must allow the Holy Spirit to correct and adjust our speech if we are to please the Lord.

However, it should be understood that there will be times in our lives when our hearts are not full of peace and we are in great need. No matter what the state of our hearts, we should always feel free to approach God and pour out our hearts to Him. He already knows our trouble, and He alone can restore us to His peace. No one understands our frailties like Jesus does. Going to Him first is the best thing we can do when our peace is shaken. Further, submitting ourselves to God ensures that we deal with our problems in a healthy manner so we continue to glorify God even in our distress.

Truly our time with God produces within us the ability to live in peace with all men as He desires. Because we know Him and He knows us, we can live differently than the world does.

*"Put on therefore, as the elect of God,
holy and beloved, **bowels of mercies,
kindness, humbleness of mind, meekness,
longsuffering;***

*Forbearing one another, and forgiving one
another, if any man have a quarrel against
any: even as Christ forgave you, so also do
ye.*

*And above all these things put on charity,
which is the bond of perfectness.*

*And let the peace of God rule in your
hearts, to the which also ye are called in
one body; and be ye thankful."*

(Colossians 3:12-15)

Paul outlines exactly how our speech can be acceptable to God in this passage. Our words should be merciful, kind, humble, and patient. These adjectives can be summed up in one word: peaceful. We should bathe our words in love and be quick to forgive. Before we take up a fight against another person, we should remember that Christ has forgiven us and reconciled us to God. Being willing to forgive those who sin against us is critical for our own well-being. It's something that Christ commanded when He taught us the Lord's Prayer. When we practice this, we have internal peace and unity, and our bond with God and the body of Christ will be perfect.

This will also outfit us to reflect Jesus in being peacemakers and ministers of reconciliation which is at the heart of our Christian walk. General McArthur has been credited as saying, "A truce just says you don't shoot for awhile. Peace comes when the truth is known, the issue is settled, and the parties embrace each other." It takes being a peacemaker to achieve that. Since authentic peace can only be attained through God, we Christians are the only people on the planet that can do this.

## Summing Up

God's peace is powerful. It sets us free from the bondage of internal strife. It sets us free from the bondage of outside disturbances too. It gives us emotional stability and self-control. God's peace helps us govern our speech by allowing us to speak like God: quietly and with self-control. As we speak forth the peace of God, we release the power of His peace in our lives and are a witness of His love and grace to those around us. Peace within grants us peace without, so we can engage the troubled world around us as peacemakers just like Jesus did.

# Chapter 5

# The Joy of Peaceful Speaking

P eaceful speech is refreshing. It brings joy to our hearts, and ministers joy to those around us too. We all want joy in our hearts, and peaceful speech brings us the joy we crave. Many passages in the Bible show us how and why this is true.

Speaking peacefully not only involves the content of our speech, but also its *tone*. Most conflicts erupt from using the wrong tone of voice instead of the wrong words, and are the result of speech that is not infused with peace. We must speak the truth, but we must do so with love and kindness.

## 1. Personal Joy Is Related to Wise Speech

> "***A man hath joy by the answer of his mouth***: *and a word spoken in due season, how good is it!*" (Proverbs 15:23)

There is a direct link between our speech and the joy we experience. Peaceful speech brings joy, while troubled speech brings heartache. Peaceful speech grants us both internal joy and joy in the company of others, so we can rejoice in the Lord. The right word at the right time brings peace and happiness.

## 2. Speaking Peacefully Is a Serious Consideration

> *"But I say unto you, that **every idle word that men shall speak, they shall give account thereof in the day of judgment.***
>
> *For by thy words thou shalt be justified, and by thy words thou shalt be condemned."*
> (Matthew 12:36-37)

On judgment day, we will have to give an account to the Lord for our idle words. There will be serious consequences if we spoke in a way that was inconsistent with the path of peace. Since the tongue has power over life and death, we need to reckon its power seriously. We may not kill somebody with our hands, but we can hurt each other badly with our words. This is a serious sin. Outward behavior is important, but the words we use are just as important. Our words will either justify or condemn us. Speaking peacefully is not optional but necessary.

> *"And as it is appointed unto men once to die, but **after this the judgment.**"*
> (Hebrews 9:27)

The author of Hebrews confirms this: We will die, and then we will be judged. God will pass judgment on our behavior and our speech. Our actions are important, but so is our speech. If we did not speak peacefully, we will have to give an account before the Lord, so we must take our speech seriously.

# 3. Speaking Peacefully Begins in the Heart

*"**Keep thy heart with all diligence**; for out of it are the issues of life.*

*Put away from thee a froward mouth, and perverse lips put far from thee."*

(Proverbs 4:23-24)

To speak words of peace, we must have a heart of peace. This proverb shows us the close connection between our words and our hearts and our lives. Diligent work keeps our hearts from perverse words. A person with a forward mouth is contrary and obnoxious. It is hard to get along with someone like this. This kind of behavior should not characterize us.

> Diligent work keeps our hearts from perverse words.

People should find it a joy to speak to us. Our hearts and our mouths should be kept in God's peace and reflect His character.

*"Either make the tree good, and his fruit good; or else make the tree corrupt, and his fruit corrupt: for the tree is known by his fruit.*

> *O generation of vipers, how can ye,*
> *being evil, speak good things? for **out of***
> ***the abundance of the heart the mouth***
> ***speaketh.***
>
> *A good man out of the good treasure of the*
> *heart bringeth forth good things: and an*
> *evil man out of the evil treasure bringeth*
> *forth evil things."*        (Matthew 12:33-35)

Jesus plainly stated that our hearts reflect our speech. A peaceful heart speaks peaceful words. Jesus illustrated this by comparing it with the fruit from a tree. A rotten tree produces rotten fruit and a good tree produces good fruit. A heart full of anger, bitterness, contempt, and deception speaks angry, bitter, contemptuous, lying words, reflecting the condition of that heart. In contrast, a heart that is full of peace, love, and kindness will speak peaceful, loving, and kind words. This is always true. A person who speaks from an evil heart is like a venomous snake. His words are deadly to others and to himself. The only way to speak good words is to speak from a peaceful heart.

# 4. Peaceful Speech Must Be Authentic

> *"Draw me not away with the wicked, and*
> *with the workers of iniquity, which speak*
> *peace to their neighbours, **but mischief is***
> ***in their hearts."***        (Psalm 28:3)

The psalmist warned us against people who speak deceitfully. The wicked say nice things to their neighbors, but in their hearts they are plotting to harm these very people. This narcissistic behavior can create many problems. Peaceful speech must always be authentic and consistent.

> *"Their tongue is as an arrow shot out; it speaketh deceit: one speaketh peaceably to his neighbour with his mouth,* **but in heart he layeth his wait.***"*          (Jeremiah 9:8)

Jeremiah gave us a similar warning. False speech does not reflect the speaker's intentions. The wicked man says words of peace but has chaos in his heart. Just like an arrow, this kind of speech can harm those who hear it. This behavior is especially harmful when so-called Christians engage in it. The world is listening to us, and watching us. When people who claim Christ as their Lord are revealed as hypocrites, the reputation of the church is harmed. Many people use the hypocrisy of people who claim to be Christians as an excuse for dismissing the gospel. Our speech and lives must be authentic.

> *"By this shall all men know that ye are my disciples,* **if ye have love one to another.***"*
> (John 13:35)

The words of Christ in John's gospel summarize this point succinctly. The world will know we are authentic Christians when we love one another. We must not only speak words of love and peace, but our outward behavior must match those words. Authentic speech and real love for others is a wonderful witness of Christ's work in our hearts.

# 5. Peaceful Speech Does Not Swear Flippant Oaths

> *"But I say unto you, **Swear not** at all;*
> *neither by heaven; for it is God's throne:*
>
> *Nor by the earth; for it is his footstool:*
> *neither by Jerusalem; for it is the city of the*
> *great King.*
>
> *Neither shalt thou swear by thy head,*
> *because thou canst not make one hair white*
> *or black.*
>
> ***But let your communication be, Yea, yea;***
> ***Nay, nay**: for whatsoever is more than*
> *these cometh of evil."*    (Matthew 5:34-37)

These verses are part of the Sermon on the Mount. Jesus provided us with the ethics of peace in this sermon. He warned against swearing in our speech. A person who insists strongly that he is telling the truth every time he talks, shows that he or she is untrustworthy. Our word should be good without the need to swear a flippant oath. We should be able to say "yes" or "no" and know that people can trust us. For this to be the case, we must follow through on our word.

We also should not make promises that we may not be able to keep. If your boss says you must put in a report by 5:00 p.m. and you swear that you will have it done when you know for a fact that you cannot finish it at the appointed time, you are not doing yourself a favor. Your boss will be angry and less likely to trust you in the future as a result. It's far better to tell your boss that you're sorry, and you cannot get the report in on time.

> *"But above all things, my brethren, swear*
> *not, neither by heaven, neither by the earth,*
> *neither by any other oath:* ***but let your yea***
> ***be yea; and your nay, nay; lest ye fall into***
> ***condemnation.****"*                    (James 5:12)

James gave us the same warning in his letter. If we swear instead of saying a simple "yes" or "no," we are at risk of falling into condemnation. Avoid casual oaths such as "I swear to God" or "I swear on my mother's grave."

# 6. Peaceful Speech Is Meek

> *"But the meek shall inherit the earth; and*
> *shall* ***delight themselves in the abundance***
> ***of peace.****"*                    (Psalm 37:11)

Meekness and humility characterize peaceful speech. Angry and selfish words are not meek. Those who use meek words will inherit the earth and experience the delight of genuine peace. Our words must remain under the control of the Holy Spirit. Such speech leads to an abundance of peace.

# 7. Peaceful Speech Proves Our Righteousness

> *"Mark the perfect man, and behold the*
> *upright:* ***for the end of that man is peace.****"*
>                    (Psalm 37:37)

We will only look at one passage to make this point, but this does not mean it is unimportant. How will people know that we are just? How will we prove that we are upright? Through our peaceful speech. Our words and actions demonstrate the state of our heart. The upright man uses peaceful words, and the wicked man use words of hostility.

**Ten Joys of Speaking Peacefully**

The seven points we examined in the first part of this chapter lay the foundation for the second half. In this section, we will look at ten specific ways that peaceful

> # Our words and actions demonstrate the state of our heart.

speech brings us joy. This joy is a blessing in our lives and can also be a blessing in the lives of others. This list is not exhaustive, but includes several important ways that Scripture tells us we can have true joy and happiness.

## 1. The Joy of Preventing Hostility

> *"A soft answer turneth away wrath: but grievous words stir up anger."*
>
> (Proverbs 15:1)

As mentioned before, gentle words can bring an end to anger and hostility. When a person lashes out in anger, we tend to respond in kind. This proverb teaches us to do the opposite. This is not merely referring to the volume of our voice either because you can say angry words quietly. Instead, this verse is concerned with the quality of our response. We want to respond to harsh words with calming words that promote peace. On the other hand, if we counter with grievous or offensive language, we will only escalate the situation. Harsh words stir up anger. The tone and general quality of our speech is important when we interact with others.

> *"**The tongue of the wise useth knowledge aright**: but the mouth of fools poureth out foolishness."* (Proverbs 15:2)

The very next verse in this passage gives further instruction. Wise people use information correctly and honestly. They do not use their knowledge and speech for evil, but for good. However, fools open their mouths and pour out whatever happens to be in their minds without consideration of its effect. This is especially dangerous in tense situations. Often fools try to get a reaction out of others because they find it entertaining. They want to stir up trouble. Peaceful people prevent hostility and promote calm instead. Preventing hostility brings us joy because it honors God and promotes our own well-being.

> *"Wherefore, my beloved brethren, **let every man be swift to hear, slow to speak, slow to wrath**:*
>
> *For the wrath of man worketh not the righteousness of God."* (James 1:19-20)

We should not be quick to speak. Instead we should become good listeners. Listening will help us to understand the perspective of the other person and create empathy. It is impossible to be hostile toward someone with whom you empathize. When we really take the time to listen to another person, anger and misunderstanding is defused all around. Instead of reacting immediately to unfair and angry words, we do better to pause, reflect, and speak peacefully. Joy will follow.

## 2. The Joy of Helping

When we live in peace, we are going to be able to help others. When we help others, we will, in turn, receive joy from this activity. Contributing to the well-being of our neighbors contributes to our own well-being.

> *"**Let no corrupt communication proceed out of your mouth**, but that which is good to the use of edifying, that it may minister grace unto the hearers."*   (Ephesians 4:29)

Paul commands us to let no corrupt communication proceed out of our mouths. Instead we should speak edifying words which bring grace to those who hear them. We are going to return to this verse at the end of this section, but before we do, let's explore what the Bible means by "corrupt communication." There are six characteristics of corrupt speech.

1. Anger
   Anger characterizes corrupt communication. We cannot speak angry words peacefully in a way that edifies those to whom we are speaking. Angry words are the corrupting opposite of peaceful speech.

2. Malice
   Corrupt speech is also malicious. The intention behind malicious speech is to hurt our neighbor

instead of blessing them. Sometimes we use malicious speech to get ahead; sometimes we use it out of pure hatred or without a motive of which we are aware. However, malice has no part in peaceful speech.

3. Bitterness

   Corrupt speech is bitter and jealous and proceeds from a spirit of covetousness. We resent the good things that happen to other people or the good things they have, and become bitter because our own lot in life seems poor by comparison. This bitterness corrupts our communication.

4. Judgment

   Corrupt speech is judgmental. It does not show mercy or grace to those who hear it. It is always ready to accuse and does not forgive. It points out the faults in people without recognizing their strengths. It cannot bring peace and joy.

5. Bias

   Corrupt speech is biased. It fails to look at things from the side of the other person. The clearest example of bias occurs in political speech. Partisan division is so great that people will defend their party even in the face of rampant immorality and corruption. Bias overrules intelligence and logic. Bias twists the truth and turns it into whatever the speaker wants people to believe. Corrupt communication is no better than political propaganda.

6. Egocentrism

Corrupt speech puts the speaker's needs and desires ahead of their hearers. Selfishness and greed are corrupt. The egocentric person chooses words that make them feel good or puff up their own pride. This speech builds them up and tears down their neighbor.

*"**Let no corrupt communication proceed out of your mouth**, but that which is good to the use of edifying, that it may minister grace unto the hearers."*   (Ephesians 4:29)

Now that we have described corrupt speech, we can return to Paul's teaching in Ephesians 4:29 and understand what this verse means. Paul wrote to let no corrupt speech come out of our mouths. Instead our speech should be good and edifying. Good and edifying speech does not have any of the six characteristics we listed above. Instead it is calm, loving, thankful, gracious, fair, and humble. These six characteristics are the exact opposites of those listed above. This speech will edify (or build up) our neighbor instead of tearing them down and promoting ourselves. Peaceful speech imparts grace and well-being. When we share grace with others, our own joy abounds. When we encourage others, we are encouraged. This brings us true joy.

### 3. The Joy of Being Heard

> *"And Adonijah the son of Haggith came to Bathsheba the mother of Solomon. And she said, Comest thou peaceably? And he said, Peaceably.*
>
> *He said moreover, I have somewhat to say unto thee. And she said, Say on."*
>
> (1 Kings 2:13-14)

Adonijah was one of David's sons. He was older than Solomon; but as we know, the Lord had chosen Solomon to be king after David. After David died, Adonijah came to Solomon's mother, Bathsheba, with a request. Bathsheba asked if he came peaceably. When Adonijah confirmed that he came in peace, Bathsheba told him to go on with what he was saying. When we come to somebody with peaceable words, they are usually more willing to hear what we have to say. If Adonijah had burst into the room, yelling, "I have something to say to you, and you better listen," Bathsheba would not have been willing to hear him out. But since he claimed to come in peace, Bathsheba was willing to hear his request.

These peaceable words had better be genuine, however. If you read further in 1 Kings 2, you will soon discover that Adonijah wanted one of his father's concubines to be his wife. Bathsheba asked Solomon, the new king, about Adonijah's request. Solomon knew that Adonijah had already tried to set himself up as king instead of Solomon before this, and saw the motive behind his words. He believed that Adonijah was trying once again to usurp the throne, so he had Adonijah and those who conspired with him put to death. Speaking the truth in peace will bring joy, but speaking deceitfully will bring grief.

## 4. The Joy of Good Relationships

> *"And David went out to meet them, and answered and said unto them,* **If ye be come peaceably unto me to help me, mine heart shall be knit unto you:** *but if ye be come to betray me to mine enemies, seeing there is no wrong in mine hands, the God of our fathers look thereon, and rebuke it."*
>
> (1 Chronicles 12:17)

Before David was made king of Israel, he had to flee from King Saul who was trying to kill him. Thirty brave warriors came out to meet David. David came to them and asked if they came to him peaceably or not. He promised them his eternal friendship if they came peaceably, but warned them of God's rebuke if their intention was to betray him. He used the phrase, "mine heart shall be knit unto you." This is a beautiful phrase that describes the intimate friendship that springs from peaceable relationships. The thirty warriors had come with good intentions, and David was overjoyed. There are few greater joys in life than close friendship with those we can trust and depend upon. Genuine friendships of peace bring great joy.

## 5. The Joy of Turning Hostility to Peace

> *"When a man's ways please the LORD, **he**
> **maketh even his enemies to be at peace**
> **with him.**"*         (Proverbs 16:7)

God wants us to abide in His peace. When we do this, it pleases Him. He increases our peace so that even our enemies make peace with us. Peace multiplies unto itself. When we act in peace, we get more peace. F. F. Bruce is quoted as saying this: "The best way to get rid of an enemy is to turn him into a friend." This is a wise proverb. The world tells us to destroy our enemies, but God wants us to pray for them and be reconciled to them instead.

## 6. The Joy of Peaceful Sleep

> *"Thou hast put gladness in my heart, more*
> *than in the time that their corn and their*
> *wine increased.*
>
> **I will both lay me down in peace, and**
> **sleep: for thou, LORD, only makest me**
> **dwell in safety.**"*       (Psalm 4:7-8)

Sleep is essential to our physical and mental health. In turn, our mental and physical health are important for our sleep. Health and sleep are intrinsically linked. The psalmist tells us that when God puts gladness in our hearts, we have peaceful sleep. We can dwell in safety and enjoy personal well-being. Peace brings joy through pleasant sleep. On the other hand, if we live in hostility with others, we jeopardize our mental, emotional, and physical health.

## 7. The Joy of Peaceful Children

> *"And all thy children shall be taught of the LORD;* **and great shall be the peace of thy children.***"*                    (Isaiah 54:13)

We all want our children to grow up in the fear and knowledge of the Lord, but we also want them to know peace and joy in their lives. When we walk in the peace of the Lord, we will pass this peace to our children. The Lord Himself will teach them, and they will have great peace. The Lord teaches children through their parents, so it is the duty of parents to teach their children to abide in God's peace. Children learn by example, so if we want them to have peace, we must live in God's peace ourselves. If we lash out in anger at others, our children will learn to do the same. If we are harsh with our children, they will be harsh with others. However, if we treat everyone, including our children with kindness, respect, and love, our children will grow up in God's peace too.

Now, you'll never find the perfect parent who has never been frustrated or raised their voice in anger to their child. All parents have failed. However, it's what we do in that failure that really matters. When we live authentically before God, our children see and understand the true process of maintaining peace and living as a Christian. As they watch us make mistakes and repent and draw from the Lord, they learn to do that too. In this way, we offer our children the chance to grow and develop in Jesus just as we do.

## 8. The Joy of Peaceful Counsel

> *"Deceit is in the heart of them that imagine*
> *evil: but to **the counsellors of peace is joy**."*
> (Proverbs 12:20)

God did not design us to be isolated or alone. We need the wise counsel of good people. This proverb teaches us that when we listen to counsellors of peace, we will have joy. On the other hand, deceitful and wicked speech cannot bring joy.

> *"A man hath joy by the answer of his*
> *mouth: and **a word spoken in due season**,*
> ***how good is it!**"* (Proverbs 15:23)

We find a similar idea in this proverb. The right word spoken at the right time is a blessing both to the speaker and to the listener. We need to surround ourselves with people who speak peaceful words to us, and we, in turn, need to speak words of peace to them.

## 9. The Joy of Reciprocity

> *"Acquaint now thyself with him, and be*
> *at peace: **thereby good shall come unto***
> ***thee**."* (Job 22:21)

When we share our peace with others, we bless them and bless ourselves. When we are kind to others, they tend to be kind to us in turn. Peace will not return to us if we speak and act with hostility. Peaceful relationships are reciprocal. We reap what we sow. The way of peace is the way of wisdom.

## 10. The Joy of Blessing God

> *"**Blessed are the peacemakers**: for they shall be called the children of God."*
>
> (Matthew 5:9)

To conclude this chapter, we will return to the Sermon on the Mount. Jesus tells us that peacemakers get a blessing from God. He blesses them because He is the Great Peacemaker. He is the God of Peace. Jesus is the Prince of Peace. What is the nature of that blessing? Peacemakers will be called the children of God. There can be no greater blessing in life than to be called God's child. Children know their status. They are loved and protected. They are blessed. We can know joy and peace because we are the children of the One who is the Source of all joy and peace.

# Summing Up

Only God brings us true joy, and peaceful speech brings us joy because it makes us a blessing to God and others. In turn, we are blessed. When we speak words of peace, we can rest, knowing that we abide in God's peace.

This is a fitting conclusion to our examination of God's peace. After Christ restores us to peace by reconciling us to the Father, He shows us through His Word how we can abide in that peace. He teaches us how to have internal peace *and* peace in all our relationships. His Holy Spirit sustains us in the path of peace and brings us joy as we speak peaceably to, and live in peace with, our neighbors. What an indescribably wonderful gift!

Even though the world is a stressful place, we can continually draw from the true peace of God that is not dependent upon the outward circumstances of our lives. It is not surprising that those who do not yet know Jesus are drawn by the peace they see so clearly in us. I pray that this book has helped you in your journey to maintain your peace with God. May you experience God's blessings as you continue to grow.

# If You're a Fan of This Book, Please Tell Others!

- Post a 5-star review on Amazon.

- Write about the book on your Facebook, Twitter, Instagram, LinkedIn, or any social media platforms you regularly use.

- If you blog, consider referencing the book or publishing an excerpt from it with a link back to our website. You have permission to do this as long as you provide proper credit and backlinks.

- Recommend the book to friends, family, and caregivers. Word-of-mouth is still the most effective form of advertising.

- Purchase additional copies to give away to others or for use by your church or other groups.

*Learn more about the authors or contact them at www.NothingButTheTruth.org.*

# ENJOY THESE OTHER BOOKS BY DAVID JOHNSTON

**Why You Were Born -**
   **A Blueprint for Discovering**
   **Your Life Potential**

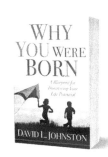

Why are you here on planet earth? Once you know why you were born you will have a new appreciation for your true self, have a known purpose in life and know why you matter. Then, and only then, can you choose a life path, a course of action and eventually a fulfilled life… no disappointments, no pressure to conform to the ideas and expectations of others. You will be free to be you, the real you.

In the second part of this book you will learn how to discover your ENA, your Embedded Natural Abilities. How tragic that some will cross the stage of time, be standing at the exit sign, and look back only to see a wasted life of insignificance. None of us can run a good race on the wrong track. "My Way," only counts if it's the right way.

Read and apply the truths of this book and you will never be a prisoner to your past or the false notions imposed upon you by others. Joy, satisfaction, and fulfillment in life will be yours.

**For Every Soldier There Is –
A Time to Kill and a Time to Heal**

*"To every thing there is a season,
And a time to every purpose under the
heaven: A time to be born, and a time to
die…A time to kill and a time to heal."*
(Ecclesiastes 3:1-3)

This vivid "Gift Book" is written for Veterans. In it they will discover the way to genuine healing.

**The Inaugural Address That Changed the World**

An Inaugural Address is a speech which marks the beginning of a new administration, rulership, or government. It is intended to inform the people of the incoming leader's intentions, springing from his or her personal values. I refer to the Sermon on the Mount as the Inaugural Address of Jesus, where he disclosed His intentions, values, policies, procedures and budget, all with the motivation of love, which is, in fact, the core of His message and mission.

*You can order these books at NothingButTheTruth.org, or
wherever you purchase your favorite books.*

## About Us - Nothing But The Truth Ministries

Dedicated to the single task of explaining the truth in its simplest and purest form to all peoples of the world.

People matter. YOU matter! Truth is the substance of all wise decision-making. So it's important to know the truth – about you, about why you were born, about every aspect of your life. Truth is wonderful, even when sometimes it may not seem comfortable.

This site is dedicated to sharing God's truth with you – truth that you can apply to your daily life; your relationships, your finances, your choices, your future.

*Visit our website at*
*www.NothingButTheTruth.org and*
*www.KingofKingsChurch.us.*

CPSIA information can be obtained
at www.ICGtesting.com
Printed in the USA
LVHW051941280122
709476LV00012B/1558

C000154430

# Camp Fo

The true story of a POW and Survivor of the
infamous Death Railway on the
Siam–Burma border

## Irene-Anne Monteiro

The Pentland Press Limited
Edinburgh • Cambridge • Durham • USA

© Irene-Anne Monteiro 1997

First published in 1997 by
The Pentland Press Ltd.
1 Hutton Close
South Church
Bishop Auckland
Durham

British Library Cataloguing in Publication Data.
A catalogue record for this book is available
from the British Library.

ISBN 1 85821 457 2

Typeset by CBS, Felixstowe, Suffolk
Printed and bound by Antony Rowe Ltd., Chippenham

In fond remembrance of
my late parents,
Emeritus Prof. E.S. Monteiro
and Mrs Una Marie Monteiro.

Eber's Dedication to his fallen comrades

Dedicated to the POWs who erected the steel bridge over the
River Kwai, Siam, during World War II.

## THE BRIDGE BUILDERS

An old man trudging along his way,
Came in the evening cold and grey
To a chasm vast deep and wide.
The old man crossed the bridge in the twilight dim,
The roaring waters below had no fears for him;
But he turned when safe on the other side,
'Old man,' said a fellow traveller near,
'You're wasting your time by lingering here,
You never again will pass this way,
Your journey will end with the closing day.'
The builder lifting his grey head said:
'There followeth after me today
A youth whose feet must pass this way.
This bridge I and my fellow POWs built,
Will welcome this fair youth in the twilight dim,
Good friend, we've built this bridge for him.'

It is as such a bridge builder, in however humble a way, that I
would wish to be remembered. And because any bridges of
hope which I have helped to build have been built in a
strength other than my own, I know that many other ordinary
people, young or old, from any nationality or culture, can
build such bridges of hope too.

C. R. Eber
20th December 1994
Singapore.

# *ACKNOWLEDGEMENTS*

I wish to thank the following for their invaluable guidance, assistance and encouragement.

His Grace, Lord Lauderdale
Mr. Cleaver Rowell Eber
Reverend Richards Ambrose
The National Heritage Board, Singapore.
The Embassy of Thailand, Singapore.
The Imperial War Museum, London, UK.
The Oral History Unit, Singapore.

From:- The Right Hon. The Earl of Lauderdale

## House of Lords

FOREWORD

Here is the story of Mr Cleaver Rowell Eber, now in his middle eighties, as retold by Miss Irene-Anne Monteiro, of Singapore. Despite his age Mr Eber still clearly recalls the sad trail of events which led him, as a prisoner of war of the Japanese, to the terrible Camp Four – Kanburi, where he was put to work on helping to build the horrific Trans-Siam railway across the River Kwai to Burma, in which many died either of exhaustion or mistreatment and consequentially failing health.

Also in my middle eighties I likewise recall the Far East war – but from a wholly different viewpoint, for in its first two years I served as a British War Correspondent with the United States, Australian and New Zealand forces in the Pacific theatre – my main part being with the United States Navy and Air Force. I still vividly recall a small trail of Japanese prisoners being brought to camp in the Solomon Islands by American G.I.s. They were not molested but in marching to the camp they *were* made to hurry up a little.

Mr Eber makes no apology for the atomic bombs dropped on to mainland Japan, neither do I – for I share what I believe must be Mr Eber's view, that without them the Far East war and all the terrors inflicted by the Japanese and the awful human horror involved would have lasted another decade at least.

By his story Miss Monteiro has made a new style contribution to the enduring moral controversy over the preservation and respect of the sanctity of human life.

# PROLOGUE

*In Oriente Primus*

Singapore's young servicemen today are in fact heirs to an age-old tradition, that of the Singapore Volunteer Corps, the Naval Volunteer Reserve and the Auxiliary Air Force.

Their proud Motto - *In Oriente Primus* (First in the East), propelled them into being recognised by Ordinance of the Government of India. When Cleaver Rowell Eber joined the Singapore Volunteer Corps it was the oldest of its kind in the Commonwealth. It had been founded as a 'private' corps.

Some of the republic's most distinguished citizens have served in its ranks. They ranged from senior civil servants, teachers and lawyers to merchants and artisans.

It was a corps which no man could join except as a private soldier. Promotion was won by merit and by examination. It holds a distinguished record of civil defence, in Singapore's history.

During World War I, the SVC was mobilised and took over garrison duties from the regular armed forces. British Europeans were conscripted for the first time in its history. Asian citizens while not subject to that law, volunteered their services in their thousands. It was multi-racial in aspect, with men from all races joining it.

In World War II, members of the SVC, as Eber recalls,

fought courageously alongside the regular soldiers of the Commonwealth forces. The SVC suffered severe losses in battle, as POWs of the notorious Death Railway in Siam and through the rigours of the Japanese occupation. It was reformed twice, attracting this time men as well as women, from all races.

The first National Service system began in 1953 with an influx of some fine young men, several of whom went on to hold high command appointments in the Singapore Armed Forces. (SAF)

When Singapore achieved self-government, it became clear that its citizens would have to play a greater role in its defence. Two regular battalions of the Singapore Infantry Regiment were formed and on active service in West and East Malaysia during the Indonesian confrontation, they gave a good account of themselves.

With Singapore's separation from Malaysia and the British decision to accelerate the withdrawal of its forces, the smallest sovereign state in Asia had to reconsider its options. It could not repel a major attack, yet it needed a military capacity that would deter such attacks.

Today the Republic has a modern Defence Force to be proud of.

# CONTENTS

# EBER JOINS THE SINGAPORE VOLUNTEER CORPS

When World War II was declared, Cleaver Rowell Eber, a Eurasian, was a young, newly qualified teacher at St Anthony's Boy's School in Victoria Street, Singapore. He had joined the staff in 1933. He was born in 1911 in Singapore. It was then part of Peninsular Malaya. Eber was newly married and he and his wife lived in a house in Yio Chu Kang. They had no children. They later adopted a boy. Life was comfortable for him and his family, and he enjoyed teaching. He was also a Scoutmaster and spent time training young boys in camps near the beach and elsewhere. He came from a large and happy family who lived in Owen Road.

When he joined the Singapore Volunteer Corps after leaving school, he never dreamt that he would one day be part of the defence force of his country.

World War II was not in fact a sudden development. It had begun at 4.45 a.m. on 31st August 1939 when Hitler's German forces marched into Poland. Britain then declared war on Germany at 11 a.m. on 3rd September in the same year, followed by France at 5 p.m. – World War II had begun.

Japanese expansionist ambitions in South East Asia began with the air attack on Pearl Harbour in Hawaii in December 1941.

Saburo Kurusu, a special envoy from Japan, had been sent to Washington DC in November 1941 to try and break the deadlock between the two countries. The United States had stopped all oil supplies to Japan. It had also demanded Japan's retreat from China.

Ten days before Ambassador Kurusu had left Japan the Japanese authorities had already decided that if the crucial talks failed, Japan would declare war on 8th December 1941. Simultaneous attacks would also be launched on the Philippines, Hong Kong, Pearl Harbour and the Malay Peninsula.

Eber, who had joined the Volunteer Force in 1930 was attached to 'D' Company of the 1st Battalion, Singapore Volunteer Corps.

*'When I was a pupil at St Joseph's Institution, I was a sergeant in the Cadet Corps. It seemed natural therefore to join the Singapore Volunteer Force when I left school. It filled me with a sense of pride.'*

He remembers vividly the excitement caused by the arrival in Singapore of the two British battleships, HMS *Repulse* and HMS *Prince of Wales*.

The British had deployed them to reinforce its defence forces here. These defence forces consisted of British, Australian, Indian and Malayan troops among whom was Eber's Volunteer Force. Their headquarters were in Beach Road facing Raffles Hotel. It was then known as the Drill Hall. The Volunteer Force not only trained there but also at Kranji, where the Japanese later landed, and also in Mandai.

Eber proudly recalls that a few years after the war he was awarded the Efficiency Medal with clasp, for meritorious service. He was a sergeant at the time.

The Straits Settlements Volunteer Corps to which he belonged had been formed before the First World War. It consisted then of only a European and Eurasian company. At that time, the Japanese were allies and had sent one or two battalions to help in the defence of Singapore, during World War I.

During World War II, the men responsible for Singapore's defence were General Sir Archibald Wavell, Supreme Commander, Far East, 1941, Major-General Gordon Bennett, Commander of the Australian Forces, General Lewis Heath, Commander of the Indian Divisions, Lieut. General A.E. Percival, G.O.C. British Forces in Malaya, Mr Tan Ah Kee, founder of the China Relief Fund and Singapore Chinese Anti-Japanese Volunteer Battalion, and Dr Lim Bo Seng, one of the leaders of the China Mobilisation Council, December 1941. When World War II began in South-East Asia, the combined overseas and local forces (consisting of three divisions, two battleships, 141 aircraft of various makes, some obsolete), were under the command of a British officer, Lt. General A.E. Percival. That fateful day, at 12.25 a.m. on December 8th 1941, the Japanese, without prior warning or a formal declaration of war, bombed Pearl Harbour. The resulting chaos at Pearl Harbour effectively crippled the US Fleet ensuring Japan complete air and naval superiority in the region.

War came to Asian countries which had not been adequately prepared to face a vastly superior Japanese army advancing relentlessly from the north, in Siam. The Japanese had imposed an alliance on the Siamese, so that they would have no fear of an attack from the rear.

For Eber and the rest of the population here, war came suddenly and brutally. A Japanese invasion of Singapore was not expected. Not only was Singapore known as an impregnable fortress, but as the Gibraltar of the East and the bastion of British might.

It was generally believed that the Japanese would need an armada and would invade from the south. All artillery installations here did in fact face south.

The local defence troops had no war experience. Eber recalls that he had spent many happy years training with the Volunteer

3

Corps. As a young boy, at St. Joseph's Institution, he had avidly enjoyed sports like cricket and hockey.

He continued his participation in sports while being trained as a teacher. Lectures were then held at Raffles Institution, Singapore's premier school. When he graduated in 1932, he looked forward to teaching in a school.

He had enlisted in the Volunteer Corps in 1930 and had regularly attended training sessions at Telok Paku near Changi.

He recalls that the conditions for enlistment were quite simple.

*'Anybody could join the SVC (Singapore Volunteer Corps) as long as you had been born in Singapore. And you could choose which company you wanted to enlist in. The "A" and "B" companies then consisted of European volunteers while "D" company, to which I belonged, was made up mainly of Eurasians. The second battalion of the Straits Settlements Volunteer Corps had three companies. "C" Company consisted of Chinese volunteers. Officers of a Chinese Military mission from China, once inspected the Chinese company of the Volunteer Force.'*

'F' Company was entirely Malay and 'G' Company were the machine-gunners, mainly Eurasians.

Volunteering at that time was great fun according to Eber. There were many who volunteered in the forces. Volunteer soldiers, sailors and airmen of several races served in the Malayan campaign. They suffered heavy casualties in it and later in prisoner of war camps like the infamous camps of the Death Railway in Burma and Siam.

Eber was one of them, but he recalls the happier times of the volunteer forces:

*'After the training sessions and the weekly parades, we would go to the club house and there meet our friends, have drinks and play billiards. We had our own magazine. It came out annually. In fact, I was instrumental in encouraging many of my friends and my old*

*pupils to become volunteers. The force was well organised. We also had our company of gunners. They managed the big guns that we had at the time. We had a First-Aid Unit in the first battalion and there were also doctors who had volunteered their services. They and the signallers were all attached to both battalions.*

*'There were three companies attached to the first battalion. I recall that the "B" Company were all riflemen; "A" Company was made up of riflemen and Lewis gunners; my own "D" Company consisted of riflemen and Lewis gunners as were "E" and "F" companies; "G" Company were all machine-gunners. The SVC had a band which played at parades. We also had a band under the baton of Sergeant-Major Galistan. In civilian life, he was attached to the Master-Attendant's Office. The band played on parade days.'*

The Officer-in-charge of 'C' Company was a Mr Yap Pheng Gek and also a lawyer, Mr T.W. Ong. They are both dead. Holding the rank of a Lance Corporal at that time was Mr Goh Keng Swee who later became Minister for Defence.

Each battalion was made up of three companies. There were also the 3rd and 4th battalion made up of volunteers from Penang and Province Wellesly. Each company consisted of about 110 men according to Eber. There were also sub-divisions or platoons. Generally four platoons would make up a battalion and each platoon consisted of about 35-40 men. The first battalion was under the command of a Lt. Colonel.

Each company had its own company commander usually holding the rank of Captain.

Eber's 'D' Company was however under the command of Major H.R. Zehender, OBE. He was succeeded by a Major Aeria. Zehender had been transferred to HQ as Second-in-Command of the 1st Battalion. 'G' Company was under the command of Capt. Henry Pennefather, but when war was declared Lt. C.A.R. Bateman, a bank clerk in civilian life, was officer-in-charge. Pennefather had retired.

The volunteers were mainly from government departments, from the schools and from the City Council, and also from the mercantile offices. They were mainly English educated as were the Chinese. In 'D' Company the older volunteers' average ages ranged from about 30 to 35 years. Many of the older members had enlisted before the First World War.

There was keen but friendly rivalry between each company. There were shooting competitions and 'D' Company won most of the prizes in such shooting competitions.

There were also many other competitions in which he took part:

*'We took part in a Warrant Shield Competition. We had to march a certain distance, about five miles, with full kit attached. Then we had to fire a certain number of rounds. As I said, in those days, volunteering was real fun and enjoyment.'*

This is to Certify that

C. R. Eber

rendered valuable assistance to MALAYA as a ....Volunteer.... during 1941–1942

Commissioner for Malaya

# *MOBILISATION*

Eber remembers that the Volunteer Corps was mobilised on December 4th 1941 approximately four days before Pearl Harbour had been bombed. He then held the rank of Sergeant. When they arrived at the Drill Hall, they were first paraded and then told to await instructions. They were also informed that they were now subject to military regulations and law. They could be court-martialled for any misdemeanours.

Camp training which was intensified consisted of weekly training sessions at Telok Paku and parades. He remembers that the food was good and that life was still enjoyable. His main job upon mobilisation was to instruct recruits in the use of a rifle, drilling, marching and using the Lewis gun.

Blanks were usually fired and training sessions held on Sundays. These were conducted at both platoon and company level. When 'D' Company was mobilised it was sent to Geylang English School which became the HQ of the 1st Battalion of the Straits Settlements Volunteer Corps. The battalion found the school empty, the pupils having been transferred elsewhere. From there, the platoons were deployed to man various posts in the area. 'D' Company had its HQ in Meyer Road in one of the old buildings at Sea View Hotel. Eber however, was sent with his platoon to a Malay School in Wilkinson Road. There they dug deep pits for their Lewis battery emplacements.

They were then joined by Malay infantrymen handling

Lewis guns. Other platoons were deployed at Tanjong Rhu right up to Karikal Mahal which is now Still Road. They were to defend the beaches and were instructed to check their gear and to be ready for action.

According to Eber morale was very good, but the atmosphere was a bit tense. He realised that all their previous training would come in useful in the event of a war.

*'It was very practical training, especially when we conducted our training in the open. Each of us had our own rifle; we all had a number attached to our names, corresponding to the number of the rifle. I looked after mine like a child; I oiled and cleaned it thoroughly. We kept our rifles at the armoury at HQ. They had to be cleaned after use and then returned to the armourer.'*

The platoon had been issued with Enfield rifles.

Although they did not undergo training outside Singapore like they do nowadays, the volunteers were also trained in jungle warfare. They went up to Bukit Timah Nature Reserve, Kranji, and certain parts of Mandai. They did not have artillery support unless the exercises were conducted at battalion level. During battalion training sessions, the two battalions would combine and the machine-gunners would lend their support. They had excellent esprit de corps. They sometimes found that while an employer held the rank of private, his subordinate in the work place would be his NCO. Everybody took things in the right spirit. They were training for the defence of their country and all volunteers took their training sessions seriously.

When he was asked if he thought his platoon was adequately prepared for war Eber replied:

*'We thought we were prepared. There were regular troops from Britain and Australia. Many had been trained for battle. What we did not expect was that Malaya would be so quickly overrun by the Japanese army. That was a shock for many of us!'*

When Eber first joined the volunteer force, the uniform was

khaki; in 1938, it was changed to jungle green. The volunteers did not wear camouflage uniform in those days.

Eber recalls that life then was peaceful.

He remembers that there was a small Japanese community in Singapore at that time, in 1941. He also taught a number of Japanese pupils who attended St. Anthony's Boys School. One of them lived quite near the school. His father was a barber with a shop close by in Victoria Street in the Victoria Building. Eber often went there to have a haircut. Japanese shops thrived in that area, in and around Middle Road. They were well patronised, by both locals and expatriates.

There was K. Baba & Co. which sold all types of goods; another was an emporium known as the 'Ten Cent Store' and the Ichigoya Co. He recalls that one of his colleagues was a Japanese lady whose name was Mrs Sakai. She was a very good primary school teacher, he says, and all her brothers were pupils at St. Joseph's Institution.

He does not remember what happened to them when war was declared. He remembers that there was respect for the Japanese during those times before the war. They were industrious, minded their own business and they were also respectful towards the local population. They kept low profiles and were mostly courteous. He does not remember any ugly incidents involving Japanese or local civilians then. He remembers patronising the Nakajima Photo Co. facing the former Raffles Institution which is now part of Raffles City.

Eber recalls that the owner, Mr Nakajima had an avid interest in various events and certain buildings in Singapore.

No one seemed to think this was unusual in any way. War was far from everybody's minds. Mr Nakajima was often seen going around with his camera in broad daylight, photographing military installations and various events. Nobody realised his real intention, which was to build up a portfolio for the

Japanese Imperial Forces.

*'We never knew he was attached to the Japanese army. But when I was a prisoner of war in Changi later, the Japanese held a victory parade. We all had to attend. It was then, to my utter surprise, that I saw Mr Nakajima wearing the uniform of a full colonel in the Japanese army.'*

There were Japanese ladies married to some Europeans but he was not aware of any clandestine activities involving them. There was, however, for a time, a significant boycott of Japanese goods. It was very noticeable, he says, in Singapore, but, as the Japanese stores sold goods cheaper than other stores, people soon returned to patronising such stores for good bargains. They were not penalised in any way by the local authorities. He himself felt no hostility towards the Japanese until war was declared and he was mobilised.

# THE JAPANESE ADVANCE

Eber realised when the Japanese army broke through Siam that hostilities had truly begun, but life in the Volunteer Force went on as usual, although training had been intensified. The government started constructing machine-gun posts which consisted of huge pillar-boxes all over the island. Barbed wire was then erected around each post. The preparations for war had begun.

According to Eber, when war broke out in Europe, it did not really have a significant effect on the local population. His friends in the Volunteer Force were hoping, along with most of the local population, that the war would end soon. In the Volunteer Corps, training sessions increased. There were more camps and participation was compulsory. Employers were ordered to release volunteers for training purposes. Salaries were paid during training and if companies could not afford to do so, the government stepped in to make up the shortfall.

When the force was mobilised on December 4th, 1941, Eber felt that 'things were really going to happen.'

However, there was still a feeling that the war would not come to Asia quickly.

While Eber and his platoon were being deployed at the Malay School in Wilkinson Road, in Singapore, two crack divisions of Japanese troops and a tank regiment landed in Northern Malaya. A little after midnight on December 8th

1941, Japanese naval guns bombarded Kota Bahru, Kelantan. Shortly before this the Japanese had landed in Siam, defeating the forces at Singora and Patani. They then pushed southwards with a field force of about 30,000 seasoned troops.

The British forces had about 140,000 troops in both Malaya and Singapore. In addition, there were countless local young men prepared to defend their country but the British did not trust them.

Admiral Tom Phillips, who was the naval officer commanding, gave orders that HMS *Repulse* and HMS *Prince of Wales* were to head for the Gulf of Siam. They were to intercept Japanese convoys landing their troops and equipment. It was a grave tactical error. The British had no aircraft to give the two warships the necessary air-cover or support. But Admiral Phillips knew it was the time of the north-east monsoons. It was during December. There were, he noticed, dark, low-lying clouds which could give the ships the necessary cover. He however, took a bad risk.

HMS *Repulse* and HMS *Prince of Wales* patrolled the Gulf of Siam for some time under the cover of the low-lying clouds. Then, while the two battleships were 180 miles from Singapore and off the coast of Kuantan in eastern Malaya, the heavy and hitherto protective monsoon clouds, suddenly lifted. It was precisely what the Japanese had been waiting for. They quickly sighted the two warships, opened fire and both battleships, crucial to Malaya's defence, sank slowly into the deep ocean. This was one of Britain's darkest days.

Two years previously, in 1938, Eber remembers reading about Sir Shenton Thomas, Governor of the Straits Settlements who had officiated at the opening of the great floating dock, at Singapore's Naval Base. Work on the great dock which was capable of receiving the larger British warships like HMS *Repulse* and HMS *Prince of Wales*, had started in 1923. The fleet

*Cleaver Rowell Eber and his wife Mabel Edith, taken 1st December 1941, before Sgt. Eber was mobilized for active duty.*

it was to serve never came.

Sir Shenton was the Governor and High Commissioner during World War II and became himself a civilian internee.

Defence strategy had for many years relied on Singapore's ability to hold out for at least three months by which time a battle fleet would have arrived from Europe. Japan, eager to make herself the supreme force in the Pacific, had been waging war against China since 1931. As the Pacific crisis gained momentum in 1941, there were considerable military reinforcements made in Malaya and Singapore, by the British.

There was a network of airfields but most of the aircraft were obsolete. There was no modern air force to carry out Britain's planned air defence scheme. No aircraft could be spared from the European battle fronts.

Propaganda built Singapore up as a mighty fortress and a great naval base but there was never an adequate modern arsenal of equipment to wage war with.

When World War II was declared, Singapore's population was 555,000 and it rose to a million by the end of 1941 when civilian refugees poured into the beleaguered city, from the north. The local civilian population such as merchants, bankers, shippers, miners and planters were told that their first duty to their country was to carry on even more efficiently and effectively with their jobs. The Imperial Japanese forces had struck early in December 1941 in a great offensive arc from Pearl Harbour to Singapore.

Dr C. Northcote Parkinson, formerly Professor of History at the then University of Malaya wrote: 'It was once predicted that the fate of the world would be decided at Singapore. It was decided at Singapore.'

It was decided when Britain resolved to leave the Singapore Base without a fleet. The British Empire was then staked on the toss of a coin. It fell the wrong side up. The order: 'Main

Fleet to Singapore' was never given.

With Japan exercising its supreme authority over sea and air, the British, with flanks exposed, suffered an ignominious defeat down the length of the Malay peninsula, capitulating in Singapore. Its great installations, barely utilised, were war-damaged, its oil depots burning, its water supplies cut and its civilian population caught in the merciless cross-fire of guns and bombs. It endured over three years of enemy occupation.

With the US Fleet crippled at Pearl Harbour, there were in fact no other battleships in the area to challenge Japanese supremacy in both the Indian and Pacific oceans. Japan could and did bring in any number of troops unopposed.

Lieut. General Percival was left with the daunting task of delaying the Japanese advance so as to enable allied reinforcements to arrive. The 18th British Division with accompanying aircraft had been diverted from the Middle East to Malaya. Help was on the way.

# MALAYA IS OVERWHELMED

The Japanese advance was swift. Their soldiers cycled or tramped through dense and leech-filled jungles, averaging about 20 miles a day. By December 12th, they had reached the much-vaunted Jitra Line in northern Kedah and by December 15th Kedah had fallen. Its forces were no match for the Japanese Imperial Army. Penang succumbed four days later on December 19th 1941.

In December when Penang fell, the Japanese gained an added advantage. With the British retreat, a top-level decision was taken to scuttle all the boats in the harbour.

Strangely, the order was not carried out and the Japanese commandeered such vessels for their own use. Using to their advantage the numerous rivers of the west coast of Malaya, they landed their troops behind British defence lines.

This meant that Lt. General Percival could no longer employ delaying tactics to keep the relentless Japanese Imperial Forces at bay.

On December 18th, Japanese forces overran Ipoh. By January 11th 1942 they were already in Kuala Lumpur, the nation's capital. Malacca yielded to Japanese forces on 16th January and on the 31st January 1942, when they landed in Johore, Lieut. General Tomoyuki Yamashita took his first speculative look at Singapore from the top of the fifth storey tower of the Sultan of Johore's palace. This was the famed bastion of

British power in the East. In the meantime, in Singapore, Eber and his platoon had been ordered to mine the beaches at East Coast Road and Telok Kurau. They undertook the task, noting the position of each mine with sketches. The platoon was then ordered to Tanglin and Bukit Timah where they had to contend with fifth column snipers.

The volunteers realised, via radio, that the Japanese forces were rapidly advancing on the island. As they waited for the inevitable, they heard stories about the British forces as they were forced towards Singapore via the Johore Causeway.

Even in defeat Eber remembers the dignity of some of the retreating troops.

*'We heard about some of the British regiments who marched proudly even in defeat. One regiment comes to mind. These were the Gordon Highlanders, a Scottish regiment, who marched proudly in defeat led by their band of bagpipers, over the Causeway and into Singapore. I felt proud to be a part of such a force even if defeat was at hand. Things began to get hot! We were being shelled every evening sharp at six o'clock. A barrage of mortars used to come over us, sometimes exploding near us. We had to duck for cover! They seemed to know where we were!'*

Unknown to Eber and the defence forces, the dreaded and experienced Japanese Imperial Guards Division which had recently seen action in China, had arrived in Southern Siam to join the advancing Japanese army.

When Eber and his platoon left the beaches for Tanglin, the 2nd Battalion of the Straits Settlements Volunteer Corps replaced them in guarding the beaches to stop any invasion by sea. The defence forces had been told by the officer commanding that they could expect either a beach landing by the enemy or a parachute landing over the airport. When the airport was bombed, Eber thought it would happen.

*'We really thought when the airport was bombed, that we would*

17

*expect to see Japanese parachutists landing there. We had been ordered to report any landing near the airport. Then, I would have brought my platoon out to to try and stop the Japanese trying to break through the perimeter. We would try our best to contain them inside the airport. We had our Enfield rifles and our Lewis guns with us. Then the Malay section had their Lewis guns. That's all the arms we had.'*

On the 8th December when Eber and his platoon were on guard duty at the Malay School, they witnessed the bombing of Singapore by Japanese Zero planes.

*'We saw the Japanese planes dropping their bombs over the city of Singapore and over the airport.'*

Eber's wife Mabel was then working somewhere in the city. He was worried about her. They lived in a house in remote Yio Chu Kang Road.

*'We had built an air-raid shelter in the grounds of our home. When I was mobilised, my wife and her mother and sisters lived there. Of course we worried about our families but my fellow volunteers and I knew that this was serious and we were prepared to defend our country at all costs and so we took our training very seriously.*

*'When we were mobilised we were informed by radio that we had to report for duty bringing our kit. We reported in full uniform. We immediately reported to Battalion HQ at Drill Hall, Beach Road and then we were deployed in our various positions. But when Singapore was bombed, the alarm went on the air. There was the sound of sirens.*

*'From where I was I could see bombs dropping over the city. The city was well lit at the time. I was on duty. We tried to count the number of planes that were flying over us. Well, we heard the bombs go off and we saw the planes. They came over quite low. I saw the red markings on the Japanese planes. I had previously identified such planes in magazines. They were the most modern Japanese planes, the Zero planes of the Imperial Japanese Air Force. I immediately reported*

*the bombings. Well, we were ready for action. I for one said: "Well, now we'll put up a show." I was in fact very relieved at that time, because I knew that our volunteers who had been training so hard were ready to go into action.'*

According to some sources, the strafing of Singapore City lasted some five to fifteen minutes. Others say that it seemed like hours.

The next morning the camp commander visited the defence forces. Eber and his men were ordered to remain on duty especially to be on guard against fifth columnists and to stop anyone suspected of carrying arms or messages. They were also told that other local defence troops were guarding the airport. Eber recalls that it was a very quiet morning on Wilkinson Road. There was no traffic; everything in fact looked peaceful and quiet when they inspected the roads around the camp. Life then at the camp was normal.

# A COUNTRY AT WAR

The volunteers carried out their routine duties of guarding their posts, cleaning their guns and resting. Food was supplied by mobile army kitchens.

From news reports, Eber and the local volunteer forces were informed of the Japanese landing at Kota Bahru and the advance of the Japanese Imperial Guards, a crack division, down Peninsular Malaya. Meanwhile, in the city, the civilian population had suffered greatly from the strafing by Japan's Zero planes. Incendiary bombs had fallen in Raffles Place. There were many casualties.

Air Raid Precaution wardens demonstrated how to put out fires caused by such bombs. Men of the Auxiliary Fire Service fought blazes caused by the bombings. There were more than 3000 ARP wardens and nearly 3000 citizens serving in the Medical Auxiliary and other services, here, during World War II. Guns to be used in the island's defence were mainly sited to repel an invasion from the sea. They were set up to protect the harbour and eastern entrance to the Johore Straits leading to the Naval Base.

Some of the fixed defences could engage targets in Johore from where the Japanese Imperial Forces launched their final assault after their ten week campaign, starting at the Malaya-Siam border. The Japanese had the advantage of being in command of both sea and air.

By mid-January 1942, more Japanese reinforcements had arrived. Two fresh divisions and a second tank division had also landed. At the battle of Slim River, Malaya, the Japanese Imperial Army fought fiercely, broke through British defences and decimated most of the 11th Indian Division.

On the 14th January 1942, the British Commanding Officer, General Wavell, arrived. He had assumed command of a newly set-up American-British-Dutch-Australian unified command (ABDA). He toured the war zone.

His visit coincided with the arrival of the 18th British Division and other British reinforcements. However, the 18th British Division would only be ready for action in mid-February. It was therefore imperative for the British to employ delaying tactics for about a month if possible, so as to delay the relentless onslaught of the Japanese.

When the Australian divisions went into action on 14th December and killed about 500 Japanese at Muar, in Malaya, General Wavell thought the chances of delaying the Japanese forces would be favourable. Subsequent events proved him wrong. His optimism was short-lived owing to the arrival of the élite forces of the Japanese Imperial Guards Division, in northern Malaya. Furthermore, many fifth-column Japanese had settled in that area and owned mines and estates there. They knew the area well. The Japanese High Command had also been well-briefed by these fifth columnists.

General Wavell told Churchill (Sir Winston Churchill, Britain's Prime Minister during the war years) that Singapore could not defend itself landwards, if the Japanese forces attacked from the Straits of Johore. Churchill was said to have been dumbfounded by this information. That the island could not defend itself landward had no more entered his mind than that a battleship might be 'launched without a bottom.'

However, morale among the volunteers under Eber's

21

command was still good, he maintains. They were even given leave to visit their families. When about a week later on February 15th 1942, the British defence forces surrendered, the Malay Peninsula was placed under Japanese occupation.

*'We were given information that a number of Australian troops in the northern part of Johore had just retreated and that they were headed towards Singapore.'*

When Eber and his men heard that the Japanese now occupied Malaya, they were shocked.

*'It was a shock to us when we heard news about the bombing and the sinking of the two British battleships off Malaya. When Malaya fell we thought, now we are in the thick of the fighting and most probably we would be told to defend Singapore at all costs. We thought Singapore would hold out. We thought there would be more troops being sent out to Singapore; more planes would come here!'*

They were banking on the propaganda put out that Singapore was impregnable and that British contingents were already on their way there.

Eber recalls meeting many of the retreating soldiers in Bukit Timah Road on February 15th 1942. At the time of the surrender, there were 85,000 British troops on the island, many of whom were in fact administrative troops. General Percival claimed that the Japanese deployed 150,000 troops in the campaign. Eber and his platoon were on duty day and night until February 15th 1942.

*'I think that in that area alone there must have been about 10,000 troops guarding the Bukit Timah approaches. The morale of the Indian and Australian troops was low. But the Scottish soldiers were wonderful 'even in defeat' marching strongly and led by their band. They were a grand sight!'*

Eber and his men were ordered to stick to their posts, defend them at all costs and be ready for any emergencies.

It was seen that the Japanese advance had been carefully

planned. It was a master stroke of brilliant war strategy which left no doubts about the efficiency and ruthlessness of the Japanese war machine.

Lt. General A.E. Percival in his book says that General Yamashita did not allow his main forces to enter down town Singapore immediately, although there were probably 100,000 troops on the island and in Johore. Japanese troops marched through Battery Road down town and Fullerton Square after the fall of Singapore. The first of General Yamashita's forces entered the town area on February 16th 1942. After the fall of Singapore Lieut. General Tomoyuki Yamashita dictated the terms of the capitulation to Lieut. General A.E. Percival, the British commander, at the Ford factory in Bukit Timah Road on February 15th 1942.

The Japanese forces had turned the dense jungle of Malaya which occupied half the land area, to their advantage. They showed their complete mastery of jungle warfare. Their troops, mounted on bicycles for rapid movement, were dressed for tropical weather. Their equipment, of the latest design, was lightweight and easily handled for jungle combat. They had studied the dense jungle terrain of Malaya well. They had been well briefed by their commanding officers.

Their soldiers carried only a ball of rice each and they lived off the land. They ate wild fruits and vegetables and drank from streams and rivers. They were tough and battle-hardened. Japanese soldiers showed the same resourcefulness in caring for themselves as the stoic Russian soldiers. Their method of jungle warfare consisted of infiltration. They had utilised all manner of local seacraft to make coastal landings behind British defence lines. So, small, highly mobile Japanese units used infiltration as their basic approach to defeat British defence plans.

The British, on the other hand, were on the defensive from

the first moment Japan had attacked. They cringed under intense Japanese bombardment. Morale was low. Eber recalls meeting many of the retreating soldiers along the Bukit Timah Road, in Singapore. He also recalls the pitiful state many of them were in.

*'We met many of these retreating soldiers coming along Bukit Timah Road. Australians who looked rather ragged. Then the British soldiers also came along and they had to remain in certain areas guarding the Bukit Timah approaches. I even remember seeing retreating soldiers of the Indian divisions in the area.'*

During the last week of January the British forces retreated into Singapore, their backs against the wall. Retreating and totally demoralised, they made a last-ditch attempt to keep the Japanese at bay. They blew up the Johore Causeway. The Japanese positioned their artillery in Johore and began close-range bombardment of Singapore.

On February 8th when Singapore was invaded, Japanese forces were met by only one inexperienced division. They could not hold back the advancing Japanese Imperial Army. Capitulation was inevitable. Communications had been practically destroyed by Japanese bombardment. Thoroughly demoralised and exhausted British defence forces could not muster the effort needed to overcome the enemy. The British defence forces together with the Volunteer Corps, were forced into a rapidly shrinking area around the city. Bombardment had also totally demoralised the local population. The defence forces had run out of supplies. Food rations suddenly became of poorer quality.

On 9th February 1942, Japanese troops under the feared General Tomoyuki Yamashita, crossed the Straits of Johore into Singapore. The Japanese Imperial Army, under Yamashita, consisted of four army divisions, supported by the Japanese Second Fleet, and the Third Air Army.

Lieutenant General Yamashita, a competent and thoroughly professional soldier, had during the 1940 campaigns, studied German war tactics at first hand. His forces were well-trained, well-equipped and had studied the Malayan terrain. They adopted tactics and strategies designed to turn all factors to their advantage.

Lieutenant General Percival was given permission to surrender. He did so on the evening of February 15th. The Malayan campaign had lasted a total of 55 days only, but it had cost the British defence forces dearly. They suffered 138,000 casualties, and 130,000 of the British defence forces were taken as prisoners of war by the victorious Japanese forces.

# CAPITULATION

Eber recalls that day clearly.

'On that day, just before we received the signal that Singapore had surrendered, my Second-in-Command, Major Webb, commandeered a tank and told me to accompany him. I drove the tank along Bukit Timah Road towards the Ford Motor Company to try and stop the advance of the Japs.

'Halfway there, we were stopped by our own troops and told that Singapore had surrendered and that we had to return to Company HQ. Well, we thought we would get some action and we were rather disappointed!'

Eber and his platoon then reported back to Company HQ. He says that there, the men's intense feelings gave way to great sighs of relief. It was a relief, as he recalled, not to be shelled repeatedly. For the first time in months he was able to sleep in peace.

The SVF was informed that the city had been severely bombed and that the civilian casualty rate was high. However, they did not at this time come into any contact with the civilian population. They were virtually isolated.

The volunteer force had been ordered to dig a deep pit and bury their rifles. Orders had come from General HQ. Eber remembers clearly the reaction of his Commanding Officer, Capt. Tuxford when news of Singapore's capitulation came through. The Commanding Officer, Capt. Tuxford just burst into tears when he was told about it. They received the news by field telephone. Then they were ordered to be assembled at Company HQ. Although the Second Battalion of the force had been ordered to be disbanded, and return to their homes, the First Battalion was ordered to remain at their Headquarters.

They did not question the order to remain at HQ. He noticed that other troops were also given the same orders to remain in HQ. There were British, Australian, Indian and the members of the First Battalion, SVC. They were to await further orders. According to Eber, nobody attempted to escape.

On February 16th, the day after the surrender, Eber and his men, who had laid the mines along the East Coast beaches, were ordered by the Japanese High Command to remove them.

They were taken in army lorries to the Katong area to defuse the mines they had laid some weeks previously. When they arrived on the East Coast, the Japanese took command.

*'We spread ourselves along the areas where we had previously laid the mines and began to defuse them. Using our sketches, we located the mines and defused them under the watchful eyes of the Japanese soldiers.*

*'It was pitch black and we had to use torches. We completed the task by midnight. We then boarded the lorries belonging to the British Army and were taken back to headquarters.'*

When they returned to HQ, they ate army rations, mostly tinned meat which they made into stews and ate with bread. There was no fresh meat.

The British in the past had claimed that Singapore was an impregnable fortress. They had presumed that it would take the Japanese over a year to reach Singapore from the north. Instead, the Imperial Japanese forces had taken barely 55 days to accomplish this.

The morale of the Japanese forces was high. They were for

the main part highly trained and experienced soldiers. Their élite Imperial Guards Division had seen action in China. Also with the dramatic success at Pearl Harbour, the Japanese forces had, in fact begun with a great advantage.

While Eber waited with his men for further orders, he often pondered about the successful war strategy of the Japanese. They had heard by radio and by word of mouth about the humiliating retreat of the British defence forces.

In retreat, the British Army had adopted 'scorch earth tactics'. Retreating southwards, they had set ablaze millions of gallons of petrol or had them drained into the soil. Docks, godowns, military installations, rubber stores, European owned firms, all had been severely damaged or razed to the ground. Looters had added to the chaos of the British Army retreating in defeat. Food was left to rot. The countryside, towns and cities throughout the Malay Peninsula became a gigantic refuse pit polluting the environment.

Upon assuming command, the Japanese Commander, General Yamashita faced the formidable task of maintaining law and order. He announced that he would take drastic action against those who disturbed public order or in any way interfered with the work of the Japanese Imperial army.

After the surrender, a military administration was set up under the direction of the general commanding the 7th Area army. He had his headquarters in Singapore. The military administration was organised under a 'Gunseikan' or President. Singapore was renamed 'Syonan' or 'Light of the South.'

It was made a special Municipality with its own mayor, because of its strategic importance.

The Japanese claimed the Malay Peninsula as Nippon Territory and it was to be annexed outright to the mighty Japanese Empire. For their enforced passivity during the war the Siamese were rewarded.

The Malayan states of Kedah, Perlis, Keletan and Trengganu, were restored to Siam by a treaty as payment for Siamese help in allowing Japanese troops easy accessibility through their territory during the Japanese invasion of the Malay Peninsula. The Japanese occupation of the Malay Peninsula will be remembered by many as one of brutality, economic hardship and Ubi-Kayu, the tropical tapioca plant which became the life-saver of the starving population throughout the Japanese Occupation. It will also be remembered because of the humiliating retreat of the British forces and also because of the inhumane way the Japanese treated their prisoners of war.

Eber himself recalls his three and a half years as a prisoner of the Japanese on the infamous 'Death Railway'. He survived but only just. It all began on the morning of February 17th, just two days after the Fall of Singapore.

Eber clearly remembers the start of his nightmare. After defusing the mines, he and his men returned to Company HQ to await further orders. He recalls that the Japanese officer in charge of operations had even thanked him and his men for defusing the mines.

# THE MARCH TO CHANGI

The day is firmly etched in Eber's mind. It was clear and sunny.

*'On 17th February, we were told to get ready to march to Changi. So we marched off at noon from the Goodwood Park Hotel where we had been billeted. We were accompanied by Japanese officers and guards. No headgear had been allowed by the Japanese. It was a very hot day but we had to leave our steel helmets behind. So, we marched hatless in the heat of the burning sun. It was a searing, afternoon heat. It was quite a long journey to Changi on foot. On the way, sympathetic Chinese came out of their houses and offered us drinks to quench our thirst. The Japanese soldiers abused them loudly but the brave Chinese took no notice of their abusers and continued ministering to the POWs on whom they had taken compassion. Many of them risked the wrath of the Japanese Imperial Forces that day. There were also minor incidents of Japanese soldiers losing their patience and slapping the civilians who had attempted to help the prisoners. Some of the bolder, local POWs even exchanged jokes in Malay with the Chinese civilians, much to the puzzlement of their Japanese captors who did not understand Malay.'*

From Goodwood Park Hotel which still functions as a hotel today, the POW contingent made its way down Moulmein Road past the Tan Tock Seng Hospital. It then made its way downtown into Lavender Street and marched to Geylang Road. There, they turned left, marched right up to Paya Lebar junction and came to Changi Road. They continued straight up the Changi Road, then passed the prison, moving directly into the Changi Military Area.

Finally they arrived at Changi which was already crowded with prisoners.

The POWs were a little tired as the heat had a deleterious effect on the expatriate soldiers. However nobody collapsed from heat exhaustion and they were glad to arrive in the restricted area. They saw that there were some British prisoners already there. Eber especially remembers the march to Changi as he saw several dead bodies lying on the ground. Their relatives and friends had probably been too scared to claim the bodies or had no idea that they had died during the bombing of the island. Most had probably died during the bombing or mortar shelling from Seletar in the north of the island. The Japanese had rained bombs on the helpless citizens.

The Volunteer Force had some difficulty finding accommodation and they had to wait in line. After some time they were told to march towards a deserted three storey building. It was built of concrete and the POWs were happy to be relieved of their packs. The building that had been allocated to them was known as Selarang Barracks. There were no beds and all POWs slept on the concrete floors.

Although Eber had noticed bomb and mortar damage along Tanglin and part of Moulmein Road, Geylang and Changi he discovered no war damage.

*'Part of the Tanglin area had been heavily damaged by bombing and mortar fire. And also part of Moulmein Road had received direct hits. However, when we came to Geylang and Changi, there was no damage whatsoever.'*

While they were marching some of the POWs had expressed the hope that their stay in Changi would be of a short duration. They hoped that soon there would be a relief force to

31

attack Singapore and they would soon be free! When asked to recollect the treatment of the POWs by the Japanese soldiers accompanying them, Eber said that they were all well armed, with fixed bayonets on their rifles.

At the beginning of the march they appeared to be quite docile. There were no major incidents between the civilian population, the POWs or the Japanese soldiers. Eber noted the bravery of the local Chinese in defying the Japanese. They continued to serve the POWs drinks and food even after being roundly abused by them. Eber thought it took courage to stand up to the Japanese soldiers who were even then noted for their cruelty.

*'The Chinese came out of their houses seeing how tired and dispirited the POWs looked. They offered us drinks and food and even had towels to wipe off our sweat! They must have felt very sorry for us!'*

The POWs were grateful for even the slightest help and eagerly refreshed themselves with cold drinks of water or munched on the food given them by the Chinese.

The captive troops had taken over an hour to reach Changi. They marched through the Changi Military Area, passing through the road that led to the prison hospital. It was the Changi Military Hospital. After waiting for some time as accommodation was being sought for them, they were then ushered to their barracks. Selarang Barracks then overlooked a large playing field. It was here that the POWs enjoyed games of football in their free time. The place was filled with British POWs who had arrived earlier. Even in wartime, life at Changi was quite peaceful. The sea was nearby and POWs could take a stroll along the beach or go for a swim. Eber remembers his morning dips in the sea which left him cool and refreshed. He also remembers attending Roman Catholic services in the chapel in Changi Prison.

He got to know a Roman Catholic Chaplain, Rev. Father Gerard Bourke who was from New Zealand. He had become a POW and has recently passed away in his homeland. Eber remembers him for his courage in the face of adversity. Several times Bourke endured harassment, punishment, torture at the hands of his captors. His fearless courage made him a war hero that soldiers like Eber remember with a great deal of affection and awe. Bourke was later interned with the other POWs on the Siam-Burma border. Eber remembers his gaunt frame and gentle eyes and above all, his courage. The Japanese treated him brutally then, tying him to trees and torturing him. Still with saintly gentleness he forgave his enemies. It impressed Eber very much.

The entire 1st battalion of the SVC had been imprisoned at Changi. Also incarcerated there were the regular soldiers of the former British Defence Forces – the 2nd battalion of the Gordon Highlanders, a Scottish regiment renowned for its bravery and war endeavours. Changi was then under the jurisdiction of Lieutenant-General A.E.Percival, former Commanding Officer of the Allied Forces. Eber and his POW friends did not see much of him, although orders were periodically issued by his officers.

Also, during this time he was worried about the fate of his wife and family. There had been little news but a lot of rumours. One rumour was that as soon as the Japanese Administration had been put into working order in the island, all local POWs would be shot for their part in the war.

Although some worried, Eber himself took these rumours in his stride. Another rumour, and one he could not ignore, was that the ship on which his wife Mabel had sailed, the SS *Felix Roussell*, had been torpedoed at sea and all lives had been lost. These were perilous times. Aboard the ship had been wives of the volunteers and other expatriates hoping to find safety abroad.

Eber lived in the hope that his family had survived the saga at sea. The SS *Felix Roussell* was a French merchant ship. It had been on its way to India when war had broken out. While on its way there, it had been hit by Japanese torpedoes. Reports filed later revealed that fires then raged aboard the vessel. There was a great deal of panic as passengers fought their way to the railings. Some, though fearful, jumped into the sea; others drowned through panic. Women and children were left stranded aboard flimsy make-shift rafts. The ship had been carrying the families of Europeans, Eurasians and the families of the SVC.

Reports later confirmed that the SS *Felix Roussell* was not only over-loaded with cargo but also took on too many passengers fleeing from fear of the Japanese. The passengers had obtained special boarding passes at Keppel Harbour in Singapore. But again according to later reports the vessel also carried non bona fide passengers and had exceeded its quota. The captain out of compassion had accepted these extra passengers; he had also sailed without an escort.

All these thoughts crossed Eber's mind as he settled into life at Changi. He remembers that Changi was a big area.

*'I remember that we went right up. I think we passed the military hospital on our left and then we came to some very tall buildings overlooking a huge playing field. We thought it was an ideal place to rest our weary bones. And we could roam, because the area was so big.'*

In fact the whole area was fenced off with barbed wire. They were supplied with food. There were special ration parties of POWs who with their Japanese guards went to collect the POWs rations. These POW food collectors had been appointed by the Japanese. They would go out of the camp and obtain rations from the village and then return with their loads. Eber and the POWs were always glad to see them return loaded with provisions. The problem of food was always uppermost in most POWs minds. There were also POW cooks and although the food was not plentiful, there was at that time sufficient for the prisoners.

They noticed that the area was completely fenced off from the civilian population. There was little contact with civilians. This was actively discouraged by the Japanese authorities. At the entrance to the camp the Japanese had posted guards with a sentry box and an off-duty tent for the guards.

Eber had received no news about his family and at that time there was no way he could obtain information about them. Then the food rations began to deteriorate.

Many meal times, the POWs were not served meat. Then there was also a shortage of fruits and vegetables. Some POWs began to develop pellagra, a disease that showed they were short of vitamins. Since security was stringent, they could not sneak out to forage in the woods for wild fruits like rambutans or papayas which sometimes grew abundantly there. So they complained about the poor food and the decreasing quantities to their Sergeant Major. These were then channelled to an officer. It was then brought to the notice of the higher officers. Despite such complaints, the food situation continued to deteriorate. The POWs who regularly collected the rations complained that supplies from the town area had dwindled. Nobody could give a satisfactory explanation but POWs noticed that their captors ate well.

However despite such hardships, morale was high says Eber. They did not go out to repair roads like some POWs near the town area, but were allowed to organise their own recreational activities. 'In Changi,' says Eber, 'quite a number of my men, myself included, got up quite early in the morning. We then showered and dressed and attended early morning service.

After that we had breakfast which usually consisted of rice porridge sometimes with a teaspoonful of sugar added.'

After their meal, the men were allocated jobs like cleaning. *There were various jobs like collecting rubbish, cleaning the area around the camp and the buildings. We had to keep the place spick and span so that there would be no complaints from the Japanese.*'

On the whole their jobs were light. They were not paid for these jobs but sometimes a Japanese guard would light up a cigarette and pass it to the POWs who would share it to the last puff. Other times, someone who had been in the food party and had gone outside the prison would come back with a small amount of cigarette butts and these would be carefully passed around. It was the camaraderie that Eber enjoyed.

Although they were in prison, they did not feel then the sense of impending doom. They still held high hopes that the allies would mount a rescue attempt and they would be out of Changi Prison free men.

Did they ever think of escape? Eber sadly shook his head when asked that question. They had their own code of honour. They were POWs and they expected to be treated with fairness. It never then occurred to them to break free from Changi. Where would they run to? The island was small and heavily guarded. Even the slightest commotion would be noticed by their eagle-eyed guards who were all heavily armed. The penalty for escaping was instant death by firing squad. The Japanese spared nobody. They ruled with an iron hand. No unruly prisoner was exempt from punishment.

# LIFE IN CHANGI PRISON

As the war casualties mounted on each side there was a race to commandeer as many beds as possible for the wounded. Japanese soldiers overran several hospitals in Singapore. They ordered the sick and the dying from their beds and gave these to their own men. Many eye witnesses say that these Japanese soldiers acted violently, throwing the sick onto the ground and even bayoneting them if they did not move fast enough. They raided hospitals for vital medical supplies which were already in short supply. They wanted these supplies for their own men. In one hospital the Japanese soldiers massacred staff and patients in cold blood. They then got rid of the bodies and moved in their own casualties for treatment. The POWs who witnessed such horrifying scenes recalled that they would never forget the brutality of the Japanese. In a mental asylum, they turned out all the patients and used the hospital for their own soldiers.

The Japanese, with their own unique code of honour never took prisoners. They saw no point in fact in keeping their enemies alive, particularly if they had been wounded. Eber himself witnessed several beatings of helpless POWs and was himself a victim of Japanese brutality.

Local hospital staff, who were exhausted from attending to all the wounded, were at times ordered at gun-point to remain on duty. Changi Hospital at that time was, according to a

British soldier, a hell-hole where anyone who could crawl would try to get away from the dying.

Eber remembers the bad reputation of Changi Hospital at that perilous time. Staff were over-worked and the wounded came in their hundreds. There were insufficient staff and poor sanitation due to the facilities being over-utilised. The hospital was over-crowded. The Japanese were not too concerned about conditions there as their own soldiers were in the better-equipped hospitals around the island. He recalls his life there. 'We were billeted according to our platoons. We put down our kits and waited for further orders.'

He remembers seeing hundreds of British and other POWs there. They had arrived earlier. The entire area was fenced up and was known as the Changi Military area. There were Japanese guards at the entrance and in the fortified area.

He recalled that there were soldiers from the Federated Malay States, British POWs and others. The FMS soldiers had come from as far away as Penang and Kedah. He remembers that the 2nd battalion the Gordon Highlanders were in Changi. There was also the Cambridge Regiment and some Australian forces. Some POWs who had suffered injuries were removed to the hospital for treatment. Helping the harassed local medical personnel in the hospital were some members of the British Royal Army Medical Corps. Some of these were young men with no experience of treating war wounds.

As some of them recalled later, the hospital was overflowing with war-wounded. Conditions were poor due to the over-crowding.

Some of the medical personnel attached to the British Army had only a year of medical training. The wounds they had to treat were sometimes horrifying. Without adequate facilities and medication they saw many of their comrades at arms die.

It was at Changi that Eber first met Reverend Father Gerard

Bourke. He was a war hero according to Sir Edward Dunlop then Chief Medical Officer of all Medical Units in Siam. But when Eber was in Changi, Reverend Bourke from New Zealand was a Chaplain for the Roman Catholics in the SVC. He later became a POW and was, together with Eber, sent to work on the Siam-Burma Death Railway.

In March of that year Eber heard that his younger brother Kenneth, who was also a POW in his company and a former employee of the Singapore Municipality, had been asked by the Japanese authorities, to report. The Municipality was then known as the Syonan Municipality. He was glad that Kenneth had been set free as he was anxious to find out about the safety of his wife aboard the SS *Felix Roussell* and also about his family who lived at 122 Owen Road, Singapore. In Changi, the 1st battalion SVC was under the command of a Lieutenant Colonel whose name Eber had forgotten.

Eber still remained in charge of his own platoon. He stayed with them and attended to their needs. Complaints were first channelled through him and then to the second in command. Then the officers of 'D' Company would meet to see if they could rectify the complaints. There were several complaints ,mainly about the food in Changi. It had deteriorated and despite complaints it did not improve.

When asked about how he felt being a POW, Eber said:

*'We were resigned to what was going to happen to us. This was something new to many of us. We had never been POWs before. And we all had the same feeling that in a few months we would all be rescued.'*

He recalls that the esprit de corps among his platoon members was good and they got on well with other POWs who were incarcerated with them in the camp at Changi.

*'Oh yes, we got on very well with the rest of the 1st battalion. I knew quite a number of them, I used to go to their building and have*

*a chat. Sometimes we would take part in quizzes, listen to talks and
have other forms of recreation.'*

While at Changi they did not come into actual contact with
the British POWs.

*'It was only on occasions like a football match that we began to
talk to them. Relations with British POWs were greatly improved
when we were sent down to various work camps in the city.'*

In Changi Prison, the POWs had become used to the
routine, Eber and his men got up rather early in the morning,
bathed, dressed and attended early morning service. Then they
returned to their units for breakfast. After breakfast the POWs
were assigned special duties. They had to clean the prison area,
collect rubbish around their area and the camp and dispose of
it. They were then reminded about the impending visit by the
Japanese High Command. They were not told who it was but
the order came through that they were to line up in full
uniform to await the visit of this Japanese General and his
convoy.

Eber remembers lining up with the other POWs along the
main Changi Road that led to the prison. There were several
Japanese guards on duty that day. It was morning:

*'And then came the convoy of military cars. And in one car I
noticed a man whom I previously knew. He formerly owned the
Nakajima Photo Studio at the Raffles Hotel building along Bras
Basah Road and facing Raffles Institution. I noticed him standing to
attention in the car. He was wearing the uniform of a full Colonel in
the Imperial Japanese Army.'*

It was a Victory Parade put on for the benefit of the POWs,
Eber believes. He believes that a grander victory parade must
have taken place in the town and that the Japanese military
convoy had then made its way to Changi. Eber thinks it may
have been General Nagasaki but he is not really sure about
that.

The visit to Changi Military Prison took over half an hour and all this time, the POWs had been standing to attention. The sun was rising in the sky and it began to get hot. In his khaki uniform, Eber felt the heat.

Although no formal speeches were given, the POWs felt it was a significant and important visit made by the Japanese High Command to impress upon the POWs their victorious assault on the island. Eber remembers that the long lines of men remained eerily silent:

*'We just waited, lined up on both sides of the road. In fact, when I recollect that day, I remember that we had to face the other way. We could not turn our faces towards the centre of the road. So there we were in the hot morning sun facing the drain, but many of us, out of the corner of our eyes saw what was happening.'*

When asked why the Japanese had made this special visit to the camp, Eber thinks that they had come to visit Lt. General Percival, former GOC (General Officer Commanding) who had his headquarters also in the Changi Military Area.

Eber recollects that life then resumed as normal. Although parties of POWs under guard were sent to collect rations, food in this camp did not improve nor did the quantities allocated to each POW. No groups were sent out to work. The camp was guarded by the Japanese. There was a guard outside the camp entrance, according to Eber. But he does not know how the total security of the prison was achieved by the Japanese. Football was a popular recreation. The POWs were allowed to move quite freely around the camp but they did not receive any news from the outside. Nor were visitors allowed.

Food was always the main topic in any discussion. It seemed always to be uppermost in their minds. But their complaints about the poor quality and quantity seemed to fall on deaf ears. The food quality began to deteriorate:

*'Everyone received the same amount. It was dished out; it was*

*received by various companies and then each company dished out its own food. We lined up with our billy cans for the food.'*

Officers and men all ate the same type of food at Changi. However, Eber does not know if the food was of a better quality for the higher ranking like Lt. General Percival and his staff.

*'The food began to deteriorate while I was at Changi. There was a lack of certain foods like vegetables. The diet was just rice with some meat and some vegetables at first. Sometimes it was a stew. We were also given tea sometimes.'*

Dinner was the same as lunch. For breakfast the POWs were given rice porridge often plain, sometimes there were bits of fish and vegetables.

He firmly believes that the inadequate diet caused many POWs to fall ill and when this happened they were quickly taken to the hospital where conditions were poor. Often, men who had been taken to the hospital were never seen again alive. Many succumbed to their diseases. But the POWs kept up their spirits. They had heard through the prison grapevine that conditions in the River Valley Camp near the town were better. Many hoped to get out of Changi. Many of the British POWs had succumbed to malaria. Members of the British Royal Army Medical Corps were on hand to help their colleagues but supplies of quinine were low and other medication non-existent. Many POWs recalled seeing their closest friends succumb to disease and death. Daily the death rate rose as exhausted doctors and medical corps officers battled with a flood of casualties. The Japanese attitude to the sick and wounded POWs was negligent according to many who survived the horrors of the prison and hospital.

Eber believes that according to the Japanese High Command, rations should only be given to those prisoners who worked. At Changi there were no Working Parties sent out to mend roads. The area was rural and had not suffered as much damage as the areas in and around the town. River Valley Camp began to become an attractive option for the POWs in Changi. Furthermore, the rising death rate at Changi gave cause for concern.

Eber was anxious, as were his comrades, to get out of Changi and so volunteered for working parties in River Valley Camp.

*'We just heard our OC (Officer Commanding) telling us that they needed a strong working party to work and live in the town area. Everyone jumped at the chance of getting out of Changi. The stench of the dying and dead was finally getting to us. Practically the majority of my company gave their names. I was fortunate (so he thought) in being selected.'*

The Japanese did not discriminate in their choice of volunteers. The entire camp was eligible to volunteer. Both the regular soldiers and volunteers stood in line to hand in their names. Apart from his company there were volunteers from other companies as well. There were many from the 'A' and 'B' companies. There must have been about 200.

Then there were also, according to Eber several volunteers from the British contingents. But the Australians were already in other camps.

One fine sunny morning, all the POWs who had volunteered to work in sites near the town area got together their meagre belongings and marched to the River Valley Camp.

They were relieved to leave Changi. They also felt that their lives as POWs would not last that long. They lived in hope of being rescued. Clandestine radio sets gave some news of a rescue and so as they marched towards the town, some of the men sang or whistled.

They had left Changi far behind and now as they looked towards the town their spirits lifted. Life at Changi, although relatively carefree, was sometimes filled with fear of catching some fatal disease like malaria, or pellagra caused by a lack of vitamins in their diets. They could forget too the groans of dying men. As Eber recalls, they eagerly looked forward to the other camp.

*'We were glad to be out of Changi; that we were really going to have more food and better living conditions. That we would be able at least to contact some of the civilians, to contact our friends and relatives also.'*

But the march to the next camp at River Valley was relatively uneventful. There were no crowds, unlike the first march to Changi. People seemed to stay away, children ran away at the sight of the marching contingent. The sun was shining brightly but somehow the mood of the lovely tropical island had changed. There were no sympathetic crowds to hand out drinks or exchange a word or two. Their guards, with nobody to terrorise or shout at, marched almost listlessly. Eber felt the wary mood of the citizens. He noticed that windows shut quickly as they passed shophouses; children were quickly called indoors as they passed houses. All this he noted and although some felt the apprehension in the air, the thought of their new home filled most of the prisoners with some hope.

After all, they needed only to spend a few months repairing roads and soon the Allies would mount a rescue attempt and the island would once again revert to being a British colony. Help they felt was not far away. Optimism was the best morale booster and their steps quickened as they neared River Valley Road where their new home was located.

Eber recalls his first impression of the POW Camp at River Valley clearly.

*'When we arrived there, we saw a good number of attap huts. They were long; there must have been easily about twenty or twenty-five of these huts. And then we saw the British POWs greeting us so we were*

*happy to have arrived there. I remember that this camp was formerly a huge playing field and that there were most probably some attap huts around it. In fact it was quite near a factory and Havelock Road.'*

# RIVER VALLEY CAMP

At River Valley Camp, the POWs were able to buy tinned provisions, bread and even cigarettes from civilians outside the camp. Electric lights had been installed in the huts and there were also showers and wash basins provided for the prisoners. They were able to bathe at any time. They were also organised into work teams which were sent to repair roads in the town area.

*'We also went to work in the town on a variety of jobs. This gave us the opportunity to scrounge around for more food and small comforts like cigarettes.'*

Together with Eber and the SVF were the FMS (Federated Malay States) volunteers and some regulars from the British regiments. The Australian POWs however were not at the camp. They had been billeted elsewhere according to Eber. The type of work the POWs did was mainly roadworks and building godowns for storage.

The conditions were in sharp contrast to Changi. He did not see any injured POWs. Everyone seemed healthy and cheerful in contrast to his other prison. The area they were billeted in had once been a huge playing field. Eber had known the area quite well during peace time. He had friends who lived nearby. It is now heavily built up and known as 'Condo Land' because of the many condominiums built there, some extremely luxurious, a vivid contrast to war time conditions.

For about two years in the nineties, Eber and his wife, Phyllis, (Mabel had died some years ago), lived in a flat in River Valley Road. He believes that the old wartime camp was just a few metres away from where his modern flat lay.

During World War II however, the site was quite different. The camp was quite near Havelock Road. There was a sawmill nearby. It was known then as the Fogden Brisbane Sawmill. Eber does not know who owned it but they were allowed to have conscripted POW labour and so Eber and his friends worked in this sawmill. Their daily task was to carry or move piles of sawn planks. When war was declared, the huge field had been turned into a POW camp and completely sealed with high fencing and gates. Japanese guards had been posted. There was a guard outside the main entrance. There were also guards posted across the road from the camp.

There was only one entrance to this camp as Eber recalls. Contact with the local citizens was strictly limited and if any civilian happened to pass along the road, past the Japanese guards, he had to stop, bow to the guards and pass on. Eber recalls that once, he saw a civilian who had forgotten to stop and bow to the guards. He was rudely recalled, a gun stuck into his face and he was ordered to bow down low. He was then pushed and slapped and finally let go. The terrified man was quite old and Eber says he ran for his life, much to the amusement of the guards.

The British Officer, who had received Eber's contingent was the Officer Commanding River Valley Road Camp. He was in charge of the POWs and took his orders regarding the POWs from the Japanese. On arrival Eber's group was allocated quarters. He remembers that even though the new quarters were sparsely furnished, they were clean. The fit POWs always feared contamination which led inevitably to catching some disease and so it was a great relief for them to find that their quarters had been well maintained. Illness meant instant repatriation to Changi Prison Hospital which they dreaded. It was uppermost in the mind of each POW that he had to keep reasonably fit and well.

Their neighbours in the camp were POWs – the Penang volunteers and the rest of the POWs consisted of the regular soldiers from some of the British regiments. The SVF were under the command of a Regimental Sergeant-Major. The SVF officers were still in Changi Prison. Eber recalls that the British POWs were members of the Suffolk, Cambridge, the Royal Fusiliers, the Gordon Highlander Regiments and some others which he cannot recall.

He believes that the camp held 5000 POWs from the former Defence Forces. There was a proper routine as the Japanese wanted to deploy several working parties at several building sites around the area. Duties were allocated each evening after the day's work was done. The next day's work schedule was then carefully noted.

However, Eber says that the SVF were not immediately put to work upon arrival at the camp.

Eber recalls their initiation into camp life at River Valley very well:

*'When we arrived, I think it was the next day, all the volunteers were called out, paraded and were told to number. So, we numbered in English until the POWs had apparently got tired of the exercise. It was then that vulgarisms crept into the accounting!*

*'The Japanese officer on duty began to scratch his head. He was clearly puzzled. He said, "No! No!, you all must learn Nippon-Go" So he made us repeat each number in Japanese after him. "Ichi," shouted the Japanese officer. It means "One" in Japanese. When the POWs heard the word, "Ichi" they all began to scratch themselves. Then he said, "Ni" which means "two". The POW all started looking at their*

48

knees.

'"San" said the Japanese officer and all the POWs strained their necks looking upwards at the hot noonday sun. "Si," continued the officer and they stared long and hard at him. By this time the officer was losing his patience. He muttered, "Go" which is five in Japanese. All the POWs to a man marched off!

'The Japanese officer then lost his temper. He abusively recalled the POWs and threatened us. He also began to abuse us. "Now, you got to learn Nippon-Go properly. Otherwise we will bash you up!" So the POWs learnt to count up to 100 in Nippon-go. We also learnt simple phrases like "Arigato" (Thank you). There were no formal lessons.'

Then they were organised into working parties and each morning after breakfast, they were sent off to these work sites accompanied by their guards. They were divided into separate working parties of regular soldiers and volunteers. They were sent to Alexandra Road for their first working stint. There was a large area of land there which Eber and his friends dubbed 'The Cabbage Patch . . .

'There we had to build godowns and we also built the long narrow roads leading to these buildings. When we had completed the job we were then sent elsewhere. Some of us were sent to work at the Fogden Brisbane sawmill at Havelock Road.'

Here, they were made to carry and sort the sawn planks. While working here, Eber was able to contact his younger brother, Kenneth, who told Eber that when he had reported to the Syonan Municipality as ordered, he was told rather rudely by the Japanese officer that he was not needed. Rather insultingly too, he was also told that he was not essential and that he was free to return home. He did this and returned to his family at Owen Road. They were overcome with joy to see him.

While Eber worked at the sawmill, he was able to see his brother quite regularly and obtain news about members of his family.

Kenneth would gather with some friends regularly at a coffee shop near the sawmill. They would cycle to the shop bringing supplies of food from home.

*'I had clothes as well as food from home. In fact my breakfast each morning consisted of bacon and eggs. We cooked these over little fires!'*

On the whole, Eber recalls, morale was high and the work force used to sing at the work site and when they marched back to camp each evening. Treatment from their captors was quite good and he remembers that the food quality at the camp was good. Each evening at 5 p.m., work stopped and they returned to camp.

There were altogether twelve or thirteen working parties belonging to the River Valley camp. Each working party was made up of fifty men. There were three fully armed Japanese guards in charge of each working party.

Their working tools were basic. They consisted of rattan baskets for carrying sand and cement and these were also used to dispose of debris from their work site. There were also long spades used for digging and other simple tools such as hammers. Eber does not recall seeing any motorised machines for building. Everything was done manually. They were supervised by their guards and sometimes received visits from Japanese officers who may have been architects of the Japanese Imperial Forces. Everything was well planned and executed by the POWs under orders from their captors.

# THE WORK FORCE

The POWs like Eber took stringent measures to ensure their good health. Sick men were immediately transferred to Changi Prison Hospital. It was something they dreaded. In the River Valley Camp there were no adequate medical facilities to treat serious cases of ill-health so the working party which was left behind to clean the camp made sure there was good sanitation.

When Eber and the POWs were sent to work at a site in Alexandra Road near Queenstown, in Singapore, they were required to carry sand and cement, dig ditches and drains. According to Eber they were involved in the actual construction of the godowns there. Eber says they had Japanese supervisors for such jobs.

*'There were Japanese soldiers who were also workmen. They supervised our work. And in fact we noticed a Japanese officer there who visited the site regularly. He was tall and spoke excellent English and he would watch us at work.'*

He believed that the godowns built there were mainly to store military or army supplies. It was close to Kepple Harbour and the rail station.

These godowns were about 150 feet long and about 60 feet wide. They were single storey buildings. There were, according to Eber, about 24 such buildings and they were all neatly arranged. All were built by POW labour. Leading to these godowns were long, narrow roads.

Eber and his comrades remained at this site until October of that year. They had left Changi in May of that same year. Each day as they left the camp, they would sing in order to lift their drooping spirits. As they marched homewards towards River Valley they would sing as they turned into Dalvey Road. It did not take them long to march there. The work site was closer to town near the beginning of Alexandra Road. The prospect of a nice hot meal, after a long day's labour made them quicken their steps. The merry songs they sang included war time tunes like 'Pack up your troubles in your old kit bag', 'Roll out the barrel' and 'There will always be an England'. Their Japanese guards did not seem to mind their carousing and good-natured banter. Quite often in this camp, they smiled.

They were happy, says Eber, that the working party had completed their quota of jobs for the day. The POWs had also as usual eaten on the work sites to save time. They were served by the mobile kitchens set up by the Japanese High Command. It was a sort of meals-on-wheels service and the food quality was quite acceptable.

The men were given basic tools to work with and after a time became quite skilful at their jobs. They dug ditches with huge changkuls or spades. They carried debris or earth and cement in large rattan baskets. They also had galvanised buckets to carry the wet cement.

There was usually a three-quarters of an hour break for lunch and another shorter break at three p.m. for about half an hour. Eber was at 'The Cabbage Patch' in Alexandra Road for most of the time. But when he had the opportunity of enlisting for work at the sawmill he immediately volunteered. He was then able to snatch time to meet his brother, Kenneth, who brought eagerly awaited news of Eber's family. There was still no verified news about his wife, however.

Thursday according to the Japanese was a 'Yasumi' or rest day. An incident which demonstrated his mother's courage happened one day at camp. His mother Mary came to visit him at the camp bringing him some clothes.

Eber was speechless when he saw her at the gates of the camp. A small, highly energetic Eurasian woman, she had walked all the way from Owen Road to the camp at River Valley Road. When she arrived at the camp. Eber recalls, she had gone up to the guard and spoken Nippon-Go, stating that she wished to see her son. She had bowed courteously to the guard and to the astonishment of Eber and the entire camp, was allowed in. No civilian had managed to do this previously. Eber admired his mother's courage.

*'I was asked to meet my mother at the gate. I was really speechless to think that my mother had so bravely done this for me. I had not expected her to come at all.'*

She had also come alone which was extremely courageous of her. An unescorted woman could have been subject to all sorts of harassment and ill-treatment by the Japanese during those dangerous times.

For Eber and the other POWs, working conditions at the sawmill were different from those at Alexandra Road. Here they were not as actively supervised. The Japanese guards let them get on with the job.

The POWs were allowed to build small items of furniture to bring back to their camp. These included tables and small benches. Some even made beds and large tables which they lugged home to camp. There were five working parties at the sawmill. Eber felt he had been lucky to get a transfer from his previous work site.

Other working parties had been sent to the docks to unload foodstuffs like rice. Although transfers were not that hard to obtain, meeting other POWs from the Allied Forces proved more difficult according to Eber. They were effectively separated from the local volunteers at the start.

The sawmill, run by the Japanese during the war, paid its workers. 'The Japanese paid us for our work there. I think it was about fifty cents a day. And with that money, we were able to buy certain luxuries and foods.'

When Eber first arrived at River Valley camp he visited the other attap huts, home to the allied forces POWs. He was very impressed by their enterprise. Despite the watchful eyes of the Japanese they had managed to operate a thriving business selling food provisions and other stores. The British POWs, according to Eber, had put up stalls selling various foods, soap and other toiletries. He thinks they must have received them from civilians on the outside. But there was danger in the air. The Japanese were by nature extremely observant. There might also have been spies eager to earn something from the guards for such information.

There were lookouts although the Japanese may not have been really aware of the thriving business run by some of the POWs. When he returned to his quarters he brought up the matter with the other POWs. Some were reluctant to come under the scrutiny of their guards. Such activity could be their undoing. Punishments were swiftly meted out and a severe beating was to be expected, if caught. But despite the danger, the SVF decided to plant lookouts and set up stalls selling tinned provisions, liquor and even beer. They obtained their supplies as some of the local POWs had good business connections.

During their lunch breaks, the POWs would disappear into small Chinese or Indian shops nearby to buy toiletries and food such as ikan bilis which was salted and packed into huge four-gallon tins. They only had enough money to buy small amounts.

They would then pack their purchases into their sacks and take them back to camp. As work stopped promptly at 5 p.m. they were able to organise some leisure time activities for their off-duty hours. In the evenings at the camp, they often played games, had talks, visited the camp library or called on other POW friends. It was, according to Eber, a relaxed atmosphere.

*'In some of the huts games like "housey-housey" and even gambling was carried on with look-outs to warn the gamblers of the approach of their guards.'*

There was also a Roman Catholic chapel where Eber attended services. On the Japanese rest day, or Yasumi, which was always a Thursday, the POWs were treated to some form of entertainment. They either had a football match or a concert in the evening.

Attached to each camp hut was a Sergeant-Major. When the working parties left each day for their worksites, these men remained behind. They received their orders from the Japanese officers. A small group of POWs also remained behind to clean the camp and to ensure the satisfactory cleanliness and sanitation of the quarters. Each outside working party was accompanied by three armed Japanese guards. Life at camp was tranquil and even dull. They were allowed to move freely about the camp.

*'Although it was fenced up with barbed wire, I sometimes used to sneak out of the camp on "Yasumi" day and visit some friends who lived on the opposite side near some old flats in River Valley Road.'*

Nobody was ever caught, but the punishment would have been severe. The POWs did not receive any mail although they were allowed to write to their relatives. There was however a radio receiver set in the camp secretly set up by the British POWs. This was never discovered although the Japanese organised periodic searches to locate it. They simply moved it from hut to hut.

The small library contained books left behind by householders in River Valley homes. It was run by the British POWs. There were cordial relations between all POWs. They played in football, rugby and cricket matches and achieved a camaraderie. According to Eber the Japanese did not interfere in this. They treated their POWs well here. They did not have morning parades nor any surprise raids on their quarters, at odd hours. The POWs were never forced to learn the Japanese language nor sing Japanese songs or participate in any Japanese festivities.

Eber recalls that all prisoners were treated equally regardless of rank. There was no discrimination between regular soldiers and the volunteers as regards duties in and outside the camp. Their guards relayed their orders to the Sergeant-Majors in charge of each hut. They were also allowed to cook their own food to supplement the rations given by the Japanese.

Eber recalls one such occasion.

*'One Yasumi or rest day we decided to cook. Together we formed a group. We had purchased "belachan" a prawn paste, some ikan bilis (salted anchovies), some onions and oil. We put this in a frying pan over a small stove and we made a very nice dish of Sambal Ikan bilis, a condiment to eat with our meals. We stored it in sweet jars and would serve it with each meal.'*

The food supplied by the camp was quite bland. Although there was always rice, the POWs often had stews made with bully beef or tinned meat. This was supplemented by vegetables. It was better in quality and quantity than Changi. As a result, nobody fell seriously ill.

News flowed between the two camps, friendships were sealed. The POWs had also received supplies of food and clothing from the South African Red Cross.

They were each supplied with a felt hat, a pair of socks, a

pair of khaki shorts and shirt, condensed milk, corned beef, cigarettes and assorted tins of meat and vegetables. These supplies had been sent from South Africa. This was the first time that POWs had received supplies and they were grateful. They had all received the same amounts.

When asked to recall life at this camp Eber said:

*'The work was hard, often back-breaking. But the food was good and so was the treatment of the POWs by the Japanese. The volunteers of the SVC consisted mainly of Europeans and Eurasians. I remember clearly the day when we were selected to go to Siam.*

*'Early in October, the volunteers were selected. There was no particular order. The Sergeant-Major just picked those he fancied. And all those who had been selected left the camp. We marched with full kit. We had been billeted together. That was the only group selected. We arrived at Keppel Road railway station with our heavy knapsacks.'*

There had been no time to inform his family. He remembers that nobody was there to see them off. He thinks that their departure must have been kept secret. They were not told of their destination nor what they would be doing once they arrived there. However, most of the POWs realised that it was significant that only Europeans and Eurasians had been enlisted. They knew the hatred that the Japanese had for them. The Japanese organised these POWs into Working Battalions. About 200 men were organised into 'D' Battalion. There were also other POWs on the train Eber noticed.

When they finally detrained the entire battalion consisted of about 1,000 POWs. The group consisted not only of the SVC but also members of the former Allied Defence Forces, mainly from the British Army. Some of these had arrived earlier. If the POWs feared and dreaded the worst, they did not show it. Both discipline and morale were good. Nobody attempted to escape. They were prisoners of war and entitled to certain considerations under the Geneva Convention.

The train was over-crowded. There was only standing room. They were packed like sardines, Eber recalls. Their long journey was northwards, often through dense jungle. They travelled through the night. They were often bitten by mosquitoes as they sped through jungle. Some of the POWs became ill from being enclosed for such a long period. The air in the trains had become stale. When it finally shunted to a stop, they were relieved to breathe fresh air again.

# THE MARCH TO KANBURI

Finally they reached their destination. The trains shunted to a stop at Ban Pong in Siam. It was some forty miles west of Bangkok, its capital. When they finally detrained, Eber recalls that the entire consignment of troops was broken up.

*'When we finally detrained at Ban Pong, some forty miles from the city of Bangkok, the Japanese authorities in charge of the troops, broke us up into smaller contingents. But fortunately for us, most of the volunteers found themselves in the same group. And we were organised into what the Japanese called, "Working Battalions". And so, about 200 Volunteers, that is, Europeans and Eurasians, were put into "D" Battalion consisting of 1000 POWs. This battalion consisted not only of the SVF members but also the British POWs.'*

Their destination was Kanburi, some 85 miles away. And during this march, due to illness and malnutrition and other diseases, many collapsed, Eber among them. They were however fortunate in having a doctor among them. Dr Pavillard had been taken POW like the others. It was he who administered an injection which saved Eber's life and to whom he says he will be forever grateful.

*'It was Dr Pavillard who gave me an injection by the roadside. After a rest, I recovered and was able to resume marching!'*

But others among the marching contingent of POWs were not so lucky. After a march of many hours the exhausted men arrived at the gates of a camp, where they were to spend the

59

night. Before they could enter the gates, a prisoner collapsed and died. They were for the most part suffering from heat exhaustion, blisters, and hunger. In addition, several suffered from dehydration.

*'We were all packed like sardines on the field. The heat was intense and we had no shelter whatsoever.'*

The British Officer in charge of these troops seeing the desperate condition that the prisoners were in, vouched to do something for them.

He said, 'I'll see that you all get a rest tomorrow.'

The prisoners were naturally grateful, but when the Japanese Commandant heard this, he immediately informed them that they were to continue their journey the following day. Weak as they were, there were murmurs of dissent among the POWs. They were being treated inhumanely and contrary to the rules of the Geneva Convention which ensured the proper treatment of POWs. The Japanese chose to ignore this, so the British Officer, angry at such treatment of the troops under his charge, strode up to the Japanese Commandant.

Boldly he said, 'My men are not in a fit condition to march. They are all exhausted. Many have blisters on their feet. They must have some rest!'

The Japanese Commandant became extremely angry. 'Do you know that I can have you shot for refusing to march!' The British OC, fearlessly replied, 'You had better shoot me now because my men are not going to march!'

And according to Eber, the POWs did not march the next day. They rested their weary bones, attended to their blisters and tried as best as they could to ready themselves for the long march the following day.

The Chief Medical Officer there was Col. Edward Dunlop. He was twice tied to a tree and told that he would be killed. He had quoted the Geneva Convention regarding the treatment of sick POWs. He was later knighted.

However, the British Officer who so valiantly came to the defence of his men was a Lt. Col. Lilley. He was much admired by the POWs for his courage and determination. He became their hero and even the Japanese whom he had defied grew to respect him. Not much is known about him but he was believed to have seen action in the Middle East and to have been decorated for valour by the British. At the time, he was Officer Commanding the Cambridgeshire Regiment. As Eber recalls, the POWs were grateful for the brief respite. They suffered greatly from heat exhaustion and the short rest revived their spirits.

After a day's rest, they felt better, contends Eber. And so the following day, they resumed marching and entered the Siamese jungle. It was dense and treacherous terrain, relatively unexplored. The boots issued were not of much help. The men felt the stony ground beneath their feet; they were bitten by mosquitoes and some had to endure insects and leeches crawling over them. Their blisters became worse. Their wounds were raw and the heat was intense.

The jungle trees were overrun by thick vines through which they had to hack a pathway. They suffered terrible deprivations and their thirst was so great that they drank greedily from muddy pools of water and afterwards suffered terrible cramps and stomach upsets. Still their captors forced them to march relentlessly forward, stopping only briefly for meals which were of poor standard. Many fell ill or succumbed to their cuts and bruises or had fevers.

Eber recalls the insect bites as being horrendous. The mosquitoes seemed to be much larger here and their bites more deadly. They fell exhausted from their fevers and from exhaustion and they tried to heal the insect bites by wrapping their heads and bodies with leaves. This gave some momentary relief. They had very little medication to overcome such problems.

When they did stop for a rest, they were only given boiled rice, weak tea or a thin, vegetable soup. It was barely enough to keep body and soul together but this was the sub-standard food that the Japanese supplied to their prisoners and the POWs had no choice but to eat it or starve to death. It was totally against the Geneva Convention, but they were beyond the reach of any such help. Their Japanese captors knew this and took full advantage of it. They were, after all, deep in the Siamese jungle far from civilisation.

Often, as he marched, Eber thought about his family, especially his wife Mabel who had been repatriated aboard the SS *Felix Roussel*. He lived in the hope of seeing his family after this dreadful war. The POWs received no mail, another breach of the Geneva Convention. They believed that their whereabouts were a secret that only the Japanese knew and did not reveal. So captives like Eber could only live in hope enduring the humiliations heaped on them by their captors. The fate of their families remained unknown.

Finally at about midnight, they arrived at the gates of the camp at Tarsao. The camp here was small and it was already overcrowded with British POWs who had arrived earlier. The night was terribly cold. They had endured extremes of heat and cold. Exhausted they fell to the ground with not even a blanket between them.

There was a meagre fire in the middle of the waste ground in the camp. Wearily some of the prisoners dragged their aching limbs towards the only source of heat on this chilly night. Eber felt himself shiver with cold. He thought he had a fever and try as he might he could not keep himself warm. 'I could not sleep due to the bitter cold. I tried to warm myself by the fire.' But sleep eluded him as it did hundreds of others on that bitterly cold night deep in the Siamese jungle. The POWs felt intensely the misery of their fate. Their Japanese captors did nothing to relieve the miserable conditions in this camp. Rations were as usual meagre. The rice was often mouldy and the dampness of the conditions did nothing to alleviate their misery.

Many of the prisoners' clothes were in tatters. To preserve what little dignity they had been left with, they salvaged gunny sacks and string and made makeshift garments from them. Some went around clothed only in loincloths, shredded of their dignity by their captors, who kept them short of everything. It was the ultimate humiliation.

Eber and his contingent were relieved to leave such drab and miserable conditions. Once again, after a stay of two days, they marched wearily from this camp. They came to a river where they were herded onto barges.

They journeyed south towards another area of desolation. It was the camp at Wampoo, deep in the jungle. It was the 17th of October. They were still a thousand strong.

*'And so, when we reached Wampoo, the Japanese chose a site which was very near the river. We immediately had to clear the site of the jungle. Work was hard and dangerous. Thorns and insect bites caused wounds which took a long time to heal.'*

Eber and his men were grossly undernourished. Many were too weak to work. But the Japanese soldiers prodded them into activity. It was slave labour at its worse.

*'We built huts of bamboo, lashed with bark and thatched with attap.'*

The huts that the POWs built, had a central gangway or passage between sleeping platforms. These were raised on either side by about 18 inches, above the ground. Each POW was allotted just enough sleeping space. In such a hut, 200 prisoners were cramped. Such was the standard of accommodation offered by their Japanese captors.

The accommodation for their captors had of course been erected previously. They were spacious and comfortable enough and beds were issued for them, a luxury that was denied the prisoners. The quality of food did not improve. On the contrary, as they went deeper into the jungle, it deteriorated.

# FORCED LABOUR

The main purpose of the Japanese in moving POWs to different locations in the jungles of Siam and Burma during World War II, was the construction of a road and rail system between Ban Pong and Thanbyuzayat which is 50 miles south of Moulmein in Burma. From the Siamese end, the road first passed through settled land. This then gave way to virgin jungle which stretched a further 200 miles. This road then passed through rocky terrain and it then crossed the picturesque Three Pagodas Pass into Burma. Then it was jungle again a few miles from Thanbyuzayat at the Burmese end.

The majority of the British POWs when they were interned by the Japanese came into this dense jungle area from the Siamese end, while the Australian and Dutch prisoners worked on this notorious stretch from the Burmese side. They were organised into six main groups called Camps which were spread some considerable distances from each other in the hinterland. Those POWs who became ill or disabled while working on the railroad, were sent to a hospital camp. Eber and his men in Camp Four were ordered by the Japanese to construct part of the road and railway for some fifty miles through this dense, virgin jungle.

According to Eber, there was in fact no proper name to identify Camp Four although it was probably located in Kanchanaburi or Kanburi for short. The camp may even have been located deep in the Burmese jungles in Wampoo. Camp Four may have remained unidentified because it may have served as the headquarters of the Japanese High Command in the area, Eber thinks. It is not marked on any map and nobody seems to know its exact location.

Eber recalls that when they left Singapore they had no officers with them as they had remained behind in Changi Prison in Singapore. They were instead under the charge of Sergeant-Majors. Each had its own. When he was asked how the other contingents of British POWs had arrived first, Eber says he has no idea. He thinks that the British POWs must have already been incarcerated at Ban Pong before them. He did not know how the British officer, Lt. Col. Lilley was put in charge of the POWs. Nor did he hear what happened to him after the war.

The POWs upon arrival at the worksite were immediately put to work to clear the jungle. It was hard and treacherous terrain. They were only given basic tools like hatchets, spades and hammers. They were expected to hack their way through jungle and rock with these simple tools. He does not recollect seeing any motorised machinery in use at that time. It was pure, back-breaking manual labour.

Due to poor diets the prisoners fell sick. In their weakened state they suffered many casualties. Nevertheless, they were forced to work. Many were weak and ill from malaria. There were no adequate medical facilities at these worksites and camps for the treatment of the sick and injured. The POWs suffered great indignities and ill-treatment at the hands of their merciless captors.

Even seriously ill men were carried on stretchers by their comrades and forced to work by the Japanese, sometimes at gun-point. Under such conditions many collapsed and died.

Work on their section of the railroad took several weeks.

Bamboo plants which had grown to heights of over 200 feet had to be cleared. Vines as thick as a man's thigh had to be hacked away using only the most primitive of implements. Also there was increased pressure from the Japanese to complete the work quickly. The pressure was intense. Men collapsed like ninepins. The Japanese, to supplement the loss of those who had died, brought in conscripted labour. At first, according to Eber, the hours though long seemed reasonable by POW standards. However, due to pressure from the Japanese High Command, this soon changed.

By February 1943, Task Work had already been introduced in all POW camps. Each POW was forced to clear away one cubic yard of earth and rock a day. This was then increased to one and a half cubic yards. Frequently, says Eber, the task would take from fourteen to sixteen hours. It was back-breaking work. Only the toughest survived.

The Japanese rest day or 'Yasumi' became a rarity. The Japanese authorities would sometimes grant a 'Yasumi' day after two weeks of heavy duty labour in the jungle. But because of the intensity of work, many POWs either collapsed, injured themselves and had to be repatriated to a camp hospital. Many became too weak to work and were often on the verge of death. Those who died were buried hastily in unmarked graves.

At Christmas however, Eber recalls being given two whole days off from work on the notorious 'Death Railway' as it had begun to be known.

Then in February 1943 officers, mainly belonging to the former British Defence Forces, were also organised into working parties. Eber does not know where they were sent to by the Japanese. It was a question of survival of the fittest. Eber, despite the odds was determined to survive. Each day he lined up with his men and set off for the jungle to complete their tasks. Gone was the light-hearted banter of the River Valley camp and the songs they used to sing.

Depression was common among the POWs and when left untreated resulted in many deaths. Men wandered into the darkness and were never seen again. Feelings of alienation were intense. Many POWs felt abandoned by their families and their countries.

There was often no mail delivered. Eber believes that news of their whereabouts was deliberately withheld by the Japanese. Families, believing them dead, stopped writing or sending food parcels via the International Red Cross. But Eber tried to remain hopeful. He believes that the routine and the hard work helped to dispel gloomy thoughts.

*'Each day we fell in on the parade ground. We were detailed by our Sergeant-major. The Japanese wanted a certain number of POWs for a specified task. After we had been briefed, the working parties then set off for their worksites.'*

A certain number of POWs with guards were left behind in the base camp. They carried out cleaning tasks which ensured the proper sanitation of the camp. Eber and the other POWs carried packed lunches but sometimes, they were allowed to cook food at their worksite, such as rice. This they supplemented with wild fruits and vegetables that they found in the jungle.

As they progressed with the work, the camp was then moved further and further into the jungle. The further they went the more isolated they became. They were allowed to mix with the regular soldiers but sometimes did not see them for days as they were involved in other worksites.

Then the Japanese began to organise mixed working parties of volunteers and regular soldiers from the Allied Defence Forces. There was no discrimination in work allocation according to Eber.

The Japanese officer who supervised them carried a metre stick and he would measure and inform them where they were to start and end a specified task. Two Japanese guards were assigned to each working party. They were fully armed.

Each Task Force consisted of about 50 POWs. When they were at the worksites, only 6-8 armed guards were left at the base camp. Later, as the work on the railroad intensified, Indian guards were introduced. They took over the duties of the Japanese guards and according to Eber these men were from Malaya and dressed in the uniform of the Japanese Imperial Forces.

Further to the north, Indian conscripted or forced labour was used. These Indian labourers, unused to such harsh conditions, suffered greatly. They quickly succumbed to cholera and died in their thousands. They were believed to be in the camps at Tonchan or Han Chee. They perished because of malnourishment and insanitary conditions. The British were then detailed as burial parties. The dead were buried in mass graves without markers.

By this time, the boots given by the Red Cross were in a bad state. There were no replacements. Most POWs began to work barefoot in inclement weather. They used rice sacks to replace their worn clothing. They began to starve as the Japanese issued 700 grms. of rice a day per man with a few vegetables. It was then not surprising that so many perished from malnutrition and other diseases, building this infamous railroad.

But Eber recalls that sometimes they were lucky. They were given quantities of salted fish, sometimes even meat like pork. But most times the rations were meagre.

*The amount can be judged from the fact that one pig was provided to feed 1,200 men! We received no milk or sugar at all. To supplement our meagre rations, we were forced to trap snakes, iguanas, catch snails or clams, and even monkeys, dog and cats. I must have eaten over 400 snakes! I enjoyed eating snakes! The flesh tasted like chicken and we usually barbecued the snake over an open fire. We also ate the leaves of the passion fruit tree and cooked wild brinjals we would find in the jungle. We once tried to capture a baby elephant! But it proved too difficult so we gave up the idea!'*

In their malnourished state, elephant meat though unusual fare, would have provided an ample quantity of meat for the men who were actually put on a starvation diet.

The Siamese, feeling great compassion for such ill-treated POWs, often supplemented their rations. They left eggs in bushes near the camp. Or they would give them tobacco, or money. The POWs would then buy medicines and food from the small village store. But there never seemed to be enough food.

Eber recorded his daily activities in a special diary he kept between October 1942 till February 1943. He says that each morning at 8 a.m. they marched to their worksite in loincloths. Because of their scanty attire they were plagued by insects, mosquitoes especially. They often took sacks so that they could bring home small animals or vegetables or wild fruits. Some took tobacco for their rest periods. During their break they would hunt for small animals or fruits and vegetables. At their breaks they would eat leftovers from previous meals or wild fruits. Eber was known as the 'Chilli King' because of his fondness for the small green chillies he found in the jungle. He ate these with rice.

After lunch the men returned to work. They worked in teams of four men at their task jobs. They were strictly supervised by their Japanese guards. Only when they had completed the specified tasks were they allowed to return to camp. Meals would be served to them from their own cookhouse upon their return.

The map shows the many camps in which the Allied Forces imprisoned by the Japanese spent, as Eber recalled, a harrowing time building the most infamous Siam-Burma Railway. This

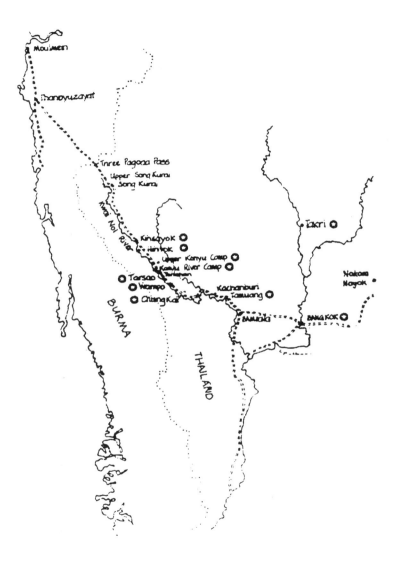

*The Infamous Siam-Burma Railway*

railway took, according to Eber, just a year to construct instead of the five years as originally estimated.

*'Death had dominion there. Therein hangs a tale of savagery, starvation and barbarity by our captors, when man's inhumanity to man matched a level equivalent to Belsen, Dachau and Auchswitz and to Stalin's starvation of the Kulaks.'*

Having overrun South and East Asia the Japanese now needed a rail link between Siam and Burma to speed communications and provide an alternative route. Initially, according to Eber, the Japanese aimed to complete the rail line in 18 months.

They wanted the job completed in ten months but had not taken into account the monsoon period. They then required enforced labour and decided to use the POWs of the Allied Forces to achieve their target.

Eber believes that overall, 62,000 POWs alone worked on the tracks under slave-like conditions using only the most basic of tools like hammers, hand-saws. He does not remember seeing any powered machines during the building. They used picks even in rocky terrain.

Sixteen thousand died, more than one in four. A life was sacrificed for every 18ft of railway track, one for each five metres in a railway that joined two systems, one in Siam, the other in Burma. Thousands died of starvation, cruelty, disease or in some cases, they simply lacked the will to live in the cauldron of hell.

He says that the Japanese were unbelievably tyrannical and generally despicable overlords. They were determined that the railway should be built. It didn't matter, says Eber how many lives were lost even if they were Japanese as well.

Their approach according to Eber was obstinately shortsighted. He complained that the food rations were meagre and the POWs fell sick because of malnutrition. To their captors sickness was anathema – the sick person did not eat and so there would be more for a fitter worker on the railroad.

Some Allied officers approached the Japanese. They told them that if the POWs were properly fed and housed the rail line would be more efficiently built. But this fell on deaf ears. Eber and the other POWs got the impression that the Japanese thought they were dispensable. They did not care how many died as long as their main objective, the building of the bridges over the River Kwai was achieved.

The POWs were fed a few grains of rice, a pale looking vegetable stew, flavoured infrequently with bits of meat and fish. Very often, maggots gave some flavour to the prawn stew served!

Eber contends that the Japanese soldiers and their officers were downright liars, very able to deny things that happened before their very eyes. He cites one example of their deviousness.

When, for example a visiting dignitary visited the camp, the Japanese would show him a truckload of food and vegetables to demonstrate to the visitor how well the POWs were fed. As soon as the visiting party had left, the truckload of food would be driven away.

Their captors were unimpressed by the contempt shown by the POWs under their care. Disease soon claimed many lives in such camps. Eber feels that he was lucky to have survived such terrible conditions. Malaria took its toll as did cholera, dysentery, tropical ulcers. Some who had lost the will to live simply wandered into the jungle and were never seen again. It was impossible to survive the jungle in their malnourished state. Japanese guards often inflicted severe beatings and tortures on the POWs which often resulted in death.

According to Eber, their captors regarded ill-health as something shameful. They starved the sick considering them as being of no use to them. They were regarded as useless and dispensable. Very often the sick were flogged to death by their Japanese guards.

Medical supplies which had been sent by the International Red Cross (IRC) would be confiscated by the Japanese for their own use. Similarly letters to the POWs and food supplies often mysteriously disappeared.

The Japanese refused to recognise the existence of dysentery among the POWs and were so fearful of cholera that they often shot POWs who went down with it. When they then ran short of men they would raid the camp hospital and force sick men to replace the dead. The sick men with blood streaming down their legs from dysentery would be forced to march to the work sites.

The guards would also kick the ulcers of the prisoners. Unused to the strain, their hearts would give out and by morning they would be dead, according to Eber who witnessed such atrocities. The dreaded cries of the Japanese and Korean guards of 'Currah' and 'Speedo' often rent the air at the work sites. Eber says that even today these blood-curdling cries still ring in his ears.

Although he regrets deeply that so many civilians lost their lives when the US dropped their atomic bombs on Hiroshima and Nagasaki in 1945, Eber felt that it meant life and freedom for the POWs on the Siam-Burma Death Railway. However he feels that it was a great pity that world-wide concern and sympathy shown to the victims of the atomic bombs in August 1945, should have deflected attention from the crimes and atrocities committed by the Japanese during the building of the railway.

## LIFE AT CAMP FOUR KANBURI

When it became dark, the POWs in Camp Four lit their candles. There was no electricity as they were deep in the jungle.

*'When it was dark, we could not do very much. We lit candles. Somebody would read or recite and we would gather around to listen. Sometimes we would sing.'*

Shift work had also been introduced by the Japanese. The POWs were ordered to do non-stop work to ensure the completion of their side of the railroad. The project had top priority.

*'When we had to do non-stop work we worked in two shifts, day and night. There was still a good feeling of camaraderie as each task force marched back to camp after the day's work.'*

For just a while, they would forget their hardships and join in the singing to lift up their spirits. They also sang to wake up the night crew who would replace them at the worksite. So as they sang their voices rose in the stillness of the night.

They had a British Quartermaster with a great sense of humour. As they neared camp he would shout; 'Today is my daughter's wedding day!' And the POWs would cheer loudly. He would then continue in a bantering tone. '$3000 I shall give away!' And they would all cheer again. Then he would say, 'On second thoughts I think it would be best to put it back in me old oak chest!' And the POWs would laugh and good-naturedly boo him.

Eber often dreamt of home. He would often wake up thinking he was home again. But it was just a dream. There was no escape from his squalid surroundings. He recalled that the worst part was the depression at being a POW miles away from home and family.

If a prisoner was caught escaping the extreme penalty, that of death, was meted out. And Eber and his comrades were in such weakened states of health that they realised they would never survive the jungle. As the work of building the notorious railroad took them even deeper into the jungle they realised the futility of escape. They were completely at the mercy of their captors.

One day however there was great excitement in the camp. The Japanese authorities had allowed the mail to be delivered. The POWs crowded around the postman, another prisoner. Eber recalls how excited he was.

*'During my three and a half years as a POW I only received six letters from my wife. So the receipt of a letter was an event not to be missed. We read them over and over again. We felt we could not eat for a week. And we put them under our pillows. Then we talked about what we would do when we returned home. And the jobs we would get.'*

But he remembers that many POWs did not receive mail. Their families had given them up for dead.

Another time when they received mail, a Japanese guard became quite friendly with some of the prisoners. He went over to a group of POWs reading their mail. He began a conversation. Eber recalls this scene vividly as it was rare for the Japanese guards to do such a thing. It demonstrated that if they were kept in good humour they behaved well. But if they became annoyed, they could easily turn nasty. That day however, the guard came over quite eager to talk. He pointed to a POW folding a letter from home. He grinned: 'You! How many wives?' he asked. The English POW grinned back. 'Five wives!' he replied. 'And how many children?' asked the guard. 'Oh ten!' replied the POW.

'Ten! Very good!' he said. 'You like Clark Gable?' continued the guard.

The prisoner nodded. 'You know him?' asked the guard.

The man smiled broadly. Quickly the guard offered him a cigarette and continued talking about the famous American film star. He was obviously an avid fan.

These were some of the lighter moments of camp life that Eber remembered. But mostly the POWs hated their Japanese guards. Many were short-tempered and treated them badly. Often even sick men were kicked and beaten for the slightest thing.

Eber's health then began to deteriorate, something he feared. One day while clearing some bamboo he suddenly collapsed. He was rushed to camp hospital. He was then treated by the POW doctor, Dr Pavillard. He recovered fully and the next day he was back at work. This was in November 1942. Again in February 1943, he came down with chicken pox. He was again hospitalised, this time for two weeks. Later he resumed work on the railway. In April of that year he was treated for tropical ulcers. He could barely walk. He had to use bamboo crutches. Finally he recovered.

In May of that same year he went down with diphtheria. This was a serious health setback. He was sent to a hospital camp at Chunkai, some miles from the river. He was away from Camp Four for almost three months. His heart had also weakened and he was no longer able to do heavy physical work in the jungle. So when the hospital needed medical orderlies, he volunteered his services. He had learnt some First Aid as a Scoutmaster in civilian life.

*'I enjoyed this work, learning how to dress wounds, washing patients and doing general nursing. My health also improved due to better food. I helped with amputations and was surprised to see that orthopaedic surgeons used ordinary handsaws to saw off gangrenous limbs.'*

All artificial limbs were made of bamboo then.

But although he enjoyed ministering to the sick he was appalled at the rising death rate. Thousands died over a period of time. In the hospital at Chungkai, there were nearly 10,000 sick POWs. He quotes that during the period of October 1943 till April 1944, there were a total of 344 deaths. One hundred and eight amputations were carried out and fifty-one POWs died.

Although upset by such figures Eber tried not to let this interfere with his work at the hospital. He was grateful that he no longer had to do manual labour at Camp Four. He heard that it had been moved further inland. After that Eber lost track of the movements of the inmates of the mysterious Camp Four.

He felt that his health had improved because the food was adequate. The hospital relied on a Chinese trader for their food supplies. He was very reliable and supplied the hospital with good quality food such as fresh eggs, fish, fruits and vegetables. Eber says that it was only in mid-1943 that POWs began to receive Red Cross supplies. They were purchased with funds supplied by the British Red Cross. Even then, Eber was convinced that some of these supplies were used illegally for Japanese troops.

He also recalls many instances of Japanese brutality. He had often witnessed many acts of aggression. Prisoners who were brought to the hospital had been subject to severe beatings and whippings. They tortured some and they often killed them by battering or using their bayonets to maim them. He often saw men being brought in for treatment. They had been either badly injured during work or they had been ill-treated by their captors. At camp sites, the POWs often did dangerous work. They were often harassed into accomplishing more than they could safely manage. This resulted in more loss of lives.

POWs in their thousands perished from injuries or ill-treatment. They died either at their worksites or in remote hospital camps. In December 1942 alone death occurred at the alarming rate of 5 POWs a day among a cohort of 1,500 men.

*'You can judge for yourself how many POWs died building this railway. The Japanese erected a war memorial to commemorate 25,000 POWs and conscripted labour who died building the railroad. These figures represented the British, Dutch, Australian and members of the SVF.'*

According to Eber the railway was completed in October 1943. And between that time and the earlier part of 1944, all POWs stopped work. They were then sent to a rest camp near Bangkok.

But one thousand POWs were not released. They were to maintain the railroad. Those who had not been selected, were then put to work building military defences for the Japanese. Work for them was probably easier, from about 8 a.m. till about 7 p.m. daily.

The Japanese authorities then decided to evacuate all the sick POWs to a new base camp at Tamuang. It was an unusual move which made Eber suspicious. They then announced that only the fittest would be selected to go to Japan. Once the selection had been made, these men were treated almost royally. They were given good food, their health built up and they were issued with new clothing. They were officially put on leave. The Japanese then informed them that they required 3000 of the fittest for the trip to Japan. As Eber recalls the group were not told why they were required. However, they listened to a speech given by the Japanese Camp Commandant. He extolled the virtues of his country and countrymen. He told them Japan was the best country in the world. Some POWs listened impassively. Others whispered derogatory remarks.

Eber, not one of the chosen, due to ill-health, noted that many were Malayans, some from Singapore. The contingent was issued with new blue uniforms and new shoes. The Japanese then made a show of these men. The camp orchestra played a few marches as they paraded. Little did they realise that they were doomed.

The contingent arrived in Singapore in July 1944. On their way to Japan by ship they were torpedoed by the US Navy. Only a handful survived. Eber later discovered that it was a Japanese experiment. The POWs had been made to undergo physical and medical tests. Most of the prisoners were Europeans with a sprinkling of Eurasians. Those specially selected were to be sent to Japanese coal mines to work as slave labour.

The health of the prisoners in the rest camps began to improve. There was also a significant drop in the death rate. At Chiang Mai Camp, the Japanese had interned 10,000 men. The previous death rate had averaged about seven to eight deaths a day. Sometimes as many as twelve a day would die. In this camp alone according to Eber, in October 1943, 257 deaths had been officially recorded. But in April 1944 only 24 POWs died, a significant decrease.

Eber believes that better health care, nutrition and the non-monsoon season resulted in the dramatic drop in the death rate. He believed that the worst for them had ended. But it may also have been that world attention had been diverted to the Japanese ill-treatment of POWs in such labour camps and that they had world opinion to contend with. But even then, it would not bring back the ones who had already perished under such terrible conditions.

*A solemn moment for Mrs Thatcher at Kranji War Memorial, Singapore, 9th April, 1985. C. R. Eber first on left.*

# THE BRIDGES OVER THE RIVER KWAI

Eber continued to work as a medical orderly in the hospital at Tamuang Camp until December 1944. His health had improved greatly. Then in that same month he was informed of his transfer.

He left Tamuang Camp with 49 other POWs for Tamarkan to rebuild the wooden bridge over the River Kwai which was adjacent to the camp. The Allied POWs built two wooden bridges and assembled one steel bridge across the River Kwai for the Japanese.

These three bridges are part of a grim episode of World War II. The building and rebuilding of them, due to Allied bombardment, cost many lives. The steel bridge has been made famous through a film entitled: *The Bridge over the River Kwai* – a Hollywood production starring the famous British actor, now Sir Alec Guinness and the American film star William Holden, who died a few years ago.

The film was based on Pierre Boulle's novel. According to Boulle, the finest British espionage agents (Force 136) which was a cloak and dagger operation, were involved. It was this group of agents who risked their lives to plant explosives on this bridge. But the actual history of this infamous bridge differs somewhat from Boulle's novel.

In June 1942, the Japanese Imperial General Headquarters issued an urgent directive. Its army was to undertake the building of a single line, one metre-gauge railway from Siam to Burma, via the Three Pagodas Pass at the Siam-Burma border to the Burma Railway at Thanbyuzayat between Moulmein and Ye. This directive issued by the Japanese High Command further stated that the project was to be completed within fourteen months or by the end of 1943, at the latest.

Work on this bridge began in October 1942 in order to meet its August 1943 deadline. This completion date was later extended to November 1943. However, the bridge over the River Kwai was officially completed by the end of October 1943. By then, thousands of POWs among them the British, Australians and Indians, members of Eber's SVC, had perished. They died building this bridge.

More than 16,000 POWs and 100,000 conscripted labour including the Chinese, Southern Indians, Malays, Eurasians, British, Australians, Burmese, Dutch and Indonesians died. Most of the deaths were due to diseases such as cholera, diphtheria, malnutrition, ill-treatment by the Japanese. Some also died from heat exhaustion and mental illness such as depression.

This infamous railroad often known as the 'Death Railway' was to provide the Japanese with an alternative to the sea route to Rangoon in Burma via Singapore and the Straits of Malacca. This sea route was being bombed by Allied aircraft and submarines.

Although there was already a road which ran from Raheng through Kowhareik to Moulmein in Burma, it was considered insufficient. Before World War II had begun, work had already started on the Bangkok-Moulmein railway. It was never completed.

When the Japanese High Command decided to complete this railroad more than 61,000 POWs were pressed into involuntary service. These prisoners had been taken in campaigns in South-East Asia and the Pacific. The victorious Japanese forces brought them into Siam and Burma to build the rail line. Eber was one of them.

Between 1942 and 1945, official records show that 30,000 British, 18,000 Dutch, 13,000 Australian and 700 US prisoners were brought in from Indonesia, Singapore and Hong Kong. In addition, the Japanese authorities conscripted labour from Malaya and Indonesia. Yet others were press-ganged into service in Siam and Burma.

This combined labour force of thousands was divided into two main groups. One group was to start work in Burma and the other in Siam, working towards the middle of this single rail track.

The metal bridge had been imported from Java by the Japanese. It was then transported by barge to Kanchanaburi and there assembled by the POWs.

When the war ended, the State Railway of Siam bought it from the Allies for about 50 million baht. The spans of this steel bridge which had been destroyed by Allied bombing were rebuilt by a Japanese construction firm as a part of Japan's indemnity after the war. The bridge is still in use today. The modernised State Railway of Thailand now runs a daily passenger service to the end of the line to Saiyok Noi waterfall, Nam Tok, leaving Kanchanaburi at 6 a.m. each day.

The building of this railway was undertaken after careful aerial surveys by the efficient Japanese, but poor engineering and the use of inferior building materials necessitated further repairs after completion. Because of Allied bombing the bridges and tracks had to be continuously repaired. This maintenance repair work needed a work force. This was the reason why Eber and his group were repatriated to Tamarkan. They were to repair and maintain one of the wooden bridges which was being continuously strafed by Allied bombers.

It was dangerous work for the POWs. Many were unknowingly killed by Allied bombers. The Japanese guards used many of the men as human shields to deter the American bombers from strafing the site. Recognising some of these unfortunate Allied POWs, tied to the spans of the bridges, the pilots then banked steeply and ceased bombing.

When Eber was sent to Tamarkan, the Japanese authorities ordered the prisoners to first build accommodation. They constructed camps at Kanchanaburi, Ban Pong in Siam and in Thanbyuzayat in Burma. The general rule was that accommodation for the Japanese soldiers was built first, followed by shelter for the POWs. Amusing tales have been circulated about the Japanese there.

One account tells of two British officers who were given a group of men, half a dozen basic tools like hammers and nails and ordered to build a hospital! The Japanese guards, noticing the army insignia worn by the British officer had assumed they were medical personnel and so expected them to have the required expertise to build the hospital.

Many of the POWs involved in maintenance of the bridges were incarcerated in Chong Kai or other such camps close to the bridges. Chong Kai camp was then one of the major camps. It is now a war cemetery.

In the beginning when they commenced repair work on the bridges, life, says Eber, was not that unpleasant. The Siamese, noted for their legendary compassion did much to try and alleviate the misery of the POWs. They donated money and food. At night, because of the lax guard system, some prisoners disguised as Siamese peasants would sneak out of camp to the neighbouring villages. However, few attempted to escape. It was a formidable task to survive in the jungle. Many were not in good health.

Many were the stories told of the Siamese kindness and

hospitality towards the POWs. The former Mayor of Kanchanaburi Municipality during the war is best known for his help to POWs. He provided food, clothing and money. There were sometimes gifts of tobacco.

Eber and the other men received news about the war through a clandestine news service set up by the prisoners. A Scottish prisoner built eight radio sets for the various camps. They were hidden in such containers as a water-bottle, a cigarette and biscuit tin; another was concealed in a bamboo yoke used for ferrying water. Yet another set was daringly sealed in the camp commandant's own radio. These snippets of news boosted their morale and kept them going even in their darkest hours.

The Siamese monks lived around the camps in Wats. These monks treated the POWs wounds and provided them with food and water. But once the work camps moved away, the monks lost contact with them.

Eber noticed that food supplies to such camps were irregular. Food rations deteriorated. Conditions worsened. Officers were paid $30 per month by the Japs.

Seven dollars was spent to supplement the mens' food and another five dollars was spent on their own food. This sum was totally inadequate. The men were unable to buy fresh foods such as eggs or medicine for the sick. They pawned their jewellery such as rings, watches, some silverware, nickel and stainless steel knives to obtain the necessary foods and medicine.

Prisoners were issued with mess kits. These consisted of a loincloth, a hat, leaky boots, khaki shorts, a tin spoon, a groundsheet, two jackets or a blanket. Some had even less.

Some became desperate enough to steal from the dead. Apart from jewellery, quinine supplies were stolen and sold on the black market. Mekong, the local whisky was sold at a hundred per cent mark-up. It was very popular.

But away from such camps, POWs maintenance crews on the railway lived for weeks on rice and salt. The Japanese claimed that it was difficult to maintain a regular supply of food to such camps. Supplies were brought upstream, along the Kwe Noi River. Fish, meat, oil, and salt supplies were often insufficient; vegetables rotted and rice was often mouldy due to the rains. The Red Cross organisation sent in its own supplies but had to contend with pilfering. POWs whose families sent parcels would often not receive them or find items missing. This added to their misery.

Because of poor sanitation and diet prisoners often succumbed to diseases like pellagra, dysentery and malaria. Often they died because there was no medication or it came too late. Eber himself witnessed the deaths of his comrades due to lack of medical supplies.

Some who suffered from diphtheria were saved by the actions of an unknown doctor. He evolved a cure during which a patient received serum from a recovered patient of diphtheria. The patient was then made to lie down and avoid any strain on his heart. This led to a quick recovery.

Periodic epidemics were always hard to control due to the primitive conditions of some camps. Cholera and plague inoculations were also not carried out stringently. Those who died of cholera were cremated.

Conditions in such camps temporarily improved from March 1944 due to world condemnation of the Japanese for their treatment of POWs. But such improvements and the turnabout in Japanese behaviour came too late. Many POWs had died.

Most of the prisoners were in main camps like Chong Kai, Tamarkan, Kanchanaburi, Non Pladuk, Nakorn Pathom. Chong Kai was rated one of the most comfortable of camps after Japanese improvements.

# THE BOMBING OF THE BRIDGES

From May 1944 until the Japanese surrendered in August 1945, many prisoners, especially in isolated camps, suffered great hardships. These were the maintenance crews who were sent to small, inaccessible jungle camps to maintain that stretch of the railway track and bridges over the River Kwai.

Such camps had been virtually forgotten. Since they were located far from the main roads and were difficult to reach, local traders rarely paid them a visit. Although there were trains to evacuate them in cases of emergency or illness, such help often came too late. Disease claimed many lives. They paid the extreme penalty.

Also, aerial bombing by the Allies took their toll. Since the completion of the railway, which now extended for 263 miles ,32,000 POWs had been conscripted to maintain and repair it, because it was the target of Allied bombing raids.

Such Allied reconnaissance flights over Burmese territory began in 1943. These were followed by periodic air raids. During the long, hot months of June, July and August 1945, the steel bridge was bombed several times. But apart from shrapnel holes, it stood firm against such repeated assaults. However, after the eight, ninth and tenth attack three of the bridge spans were destroyed. These were on the Kanchanaburi side. When World War II ended, the bridge was repaired and the smaller spans were replaced by two larger spans.

Eber recalls the day when he and his group were sent to such a camp as a maintenance crew. They were sent to the camp at Tamarkan to repair the bridge. They discovered that they had to rebuild part of the wooden bridge spanning the river. As Eber recalls this had been blown up by the Americans.

*'This wooden bridge had been blown up by American B29 bombers. It was located about 50 yards from the steel bridge erected by Allied POWs in 1943. But this bridge had received slight damage then during the bombing raids. We rebuilt it in just under a month. We worked from about 5 a.m. till about 7 p.m. daily.'*

There were many assaults on these bridges. The camp he was in was situated close to the bridges, the railway lines and the 'ack-ack' guns of the Japanese forces. The POWs had dug narrow trenches in which to shelter. They rarely slept well. They received four or five alarms each day. Their nerves were completely shattered by such air-raids.

*'Once, twenty-four B-29 planes of the US Air Force bombed and smashed Japanese artillery emplacements killing a great number of the enemy.'*

As many of these camps were situated next to tracks and near the bridges over the river, the Allied air raids also caused the deaths of many of the hapless POWs. In some camps, according to Eber, they were not even allowed to dig trenches for their own safety. Their only shelters were the flimsy bamboo huts. And again, contrary to the Geneva Convention, they were not allowed to display the symbol of a POW Camp - the flag with a white triangle on a blue background. In some camps, the Japanese camp commandants in an attempt to stop or deter Allied bombings, forced their prisoners to climb trees as lookouts. They had to look out for planes and warn the camp. Many POWs were killed. Towards the end of the war however, Eber recalls reading that Allied parachutists landed 23 miles from the POW camps in Kanchanaburi without the

Japanese being aware of such a drop.

Eber and his fellow prisoners continued their repairs on the bridge. Finally, after repeated efforts the Japanese authorities gave up all attempts to repair both bridges. The Allied bombers had done irreparable damage. Eber and his group were happy to return to Tamuang. Many POWs left with shattered nerves, some never fully recovered from their ordeal.

On March 24th 1945, Eber left Tamuang in a group of 200 POWs.

*'We travelled in open trucks to Bangkok. Then, we marched one hundred miles north-east to a new camp called Nakhon Nayok or Namkomnai where there were already 400 other POWs. We were later joined by another 1000 from the camp in Tamwan.'*

This group of Allied POWs were regrouped and renamed. They were to be known as 'Group 5'. They were also given new instructions. They were to join working parties to build roads and fortifications around the district. Eber was pleased to note that food supplies in this camp were regular and their rations were adequate. It made him happier although his happiness was short-lived.

With this new group, the Japanese had organised a march up country. It was the most gruelling march that Eber had ever experienced.

*'On the morning of 3rd June 1945, I was in this party of 800 POWs. We left Nakkhomnai Camp for an unknown destination. This march only ended on August 17th at Phitsanluk, after 600 kilometres.'*

It was the most arduous march the prisoners had ever been on.

They marched with full kit, and in addition pushed two heavily laden carts filled with stores and guards' kits, through narrow jungle trails, over hills and valleys and often through dense jungle terrain.

Seven men died during this march. Prisoners had to contend with meagre food rations and inadequate medical supplies. They succumbed to malaria, tropical ulcers, dysentery and beri-beri.

During this march the POWs were secretly informed by the friendly Siamese that the war had ended. Thirty-eight prisoners succeeded in escaping. Eber, due to ill-health decided against the idea. He thought that he would not have survived the rigours of the jungle.

On the first evening of this gruesome march the contingent spent the night in a paddy field. When they arrived, they were not allowed to erect temporary bamboo shelters. The weather had been inclement and the POWs huddled together for warmth under dark skies.

That night, there was a tropical storm, the worst Eber had

## Memorandum.

| From | | 31st October 19 66. |
|---|---|---|
| THE BROTHER DIRECTOR. | | To ....The Minister of Education, |
| **St. Joseph's Institution.** | | Ministry of Education, |
| SINGAPORE. | | Singapore. |
| Phone 33968 | | |

Mr. C.R.Eber's record of service is a most impressive one. Besides classroom work which he has invariably carried out both conscientiously and enthusiastically,he has been Sports Secretary of Primary as well as Secondary Schools for the past 29 years; for 39 years,for the benefit of the school he has put to good use his ability to play the piano;for 7 years he was in charge of the Wolf Cubs Pack;in 1950 as Manager-Coach,he led the Singapore Schools Cricket Team to Western Australia;he works actively on the Newton District Sports Council;while last year he organised the Primary Swimming Carnival for the Newton District.

Despite his age,Mr. Eber has lost none of the sprightliness and energy of youth.He is a man who is unreservedly dedicated to his work,a man who allows no other interests to distract him from his love-teaching.

May I presume to request that his application for extension of service receive your favourable consideration?

Very respectfully yours,

c.c. Director of Education.

BT. JOSEPH'S INSTITUTION

Bro. Justin
Director.

91

ever experienced. It was an electrical storm accompanied by very heavy rain. It became very cold and the prisoners began exercising just to keep warm. Eber recalls the scene vividly. Hundreds of dampened POWs illuminated by the thunderous flashes of lightning, could be seen performing physical jerks and singing loudly to keep up their spirits. The camp commandant, Lt. Daimin, a humourless Japanese officer, attempted to stop the prisoners from their antics, from the warmth of his own shelter. He failed and the prisoners continued with their impromptu exercises. Lt. Daimin often ordered his soldiers to ill-treat the prisoners.

They were subjected to beatings and whippings, and other indignities. Eber was one of his victims.

*'It was during this time that I received a severe bashing which knocked me out. I also lost several teeth as a result of this beating!'*

He received no dental treatment but was helped by other POWs.

Lt. Daimin was also guilty of handing out orders which resulted in several POWs being unjustly punished and some were even maimed. Eber's health and that of the other POWs was also severely strained due to this long march. Their rations were also inadequate and they often had to survive on weak tea, rice porridge. There was rarely any meat. In this weakened condition it was difficult for any POW to have survived the Siamese jungle. Escape was always on their minds but they wisely understood the constraints they were under. Only the fittest attempted to escape. Some were caught and were shot by a Japanese firing squad. According to Eber, Lt. Daimin's severe treatment of the POWs was the standard behaviour of such commandants put in charge of the virtually helpless prisoners.

# LIBERATION

It was at Phitsanluk that Eber and his fellow prisoners were officially told by the Japanese that the war was over. However, they had to wait for some weeks before they were repatriated to the safer environment of a British camp. While awaiting their transfer, Eber recalls that the Japanese treated them well. They were issued with kits, blankets and food supplies.

It was on August 21st that the prisoners were repatriated, together with their sick colleagues. They boarded trains and headed for Takuri Camp about one hundred and twenty miles south. It was here that for the first time since war had been declared that they saw the British flag flying steadily in the breeze. They cheered their hearts out and for many it was the official sign that finally the war had ended. Their terrible ordeal was over.

Their day of liberation had arrived according to Eber. Three and a half years of darkness and sheer agony had passed.

*'We saw the new dawn, bringing with it deliverance from danger and anxiety.'*

He recalls that his company had lost 14 men. The infamous Death Railway had claimed over thirty thousand lives. In the death camps, they had died in their thousands from malnutrition, ill-treatment, starvation and tropical diseases.

When tired, thirsty soldiers drank unknowingly from puddles and nearby streams, cholera and dysentery claimed them. It had been a war full of human misery and desolation.

As Eber patiently awaited repatriation he remembered how he and his fellow prisoners had dreaded tropical ulcers. Thousands fell victim to this dreadful malady he says. He recalls that within 48 hours, a small sore would develop into an unsightly septic ulcer. Poor sanitation, contaminated food and water supplies added to their grave discomfort.

When death had claimed many lives he remembered somewhat bitterly how their Japanese captors had increased shift duties. The men were, according to Eber, driven until they dropped.

But the POWs, for all their hardships, continued to have a high morale. They were never down-hearted Eber recalled. He remembered in particular the courage and leadership displayed by their officers, particularly the medical orderlies during those stressful times.

Not to be forgotten were the chaplains who though tormented and sometimes ill-treated by their captors continued to render invaluable spiritual services to the men. Eber remembered with gladness the Christmas festivities arranged by the POWs and chaplains who brought joy for a short time.

As they awaited repatriation, the Red Cross dropped food supplies over the camps, from low-flying Dakotas. Later some smaller aircraft arrived at a new landing strip which had been built by POW labour. They too brought much sought-after food and medical supplies. Badly injured prisoners were treated and they were issued with such luxuries as English cigarettes, books, magazines, newspapers.

Eber relishes the memory of his first English cigarette. The food had improved and he felt happy. 'We were allowed to send telegrams and write letters to our families,' he remembers. He wrote to his wife Mabel to inform her of his impending release. But because of an outbreak of smallpox in a camp lower down river, Eber and his fellow prisoners remained at Takuri Camp for two weeks. The weather also proved to be inclement with low lying cloud and poor visibility so all flights had to be cancelled. As he recalls, the general evacuation of all POWs did not take place until late September.

He was excited about meeting his family after all those years away. He lay under the stars at night wondering what conditions would be like at home. He had not been given any reliable news reports for years. The Japanese had successfully blocked any real news from coming through to the camps under their command. Eber and prisoners like him could only hope and wait.

*'I left Takuri Camp on the 20th September. In a few hours our army plane had landed in the military aerodrome of Mongaladon. The airstrip was three and a half miles north of Rangoon.'*

After they had landed, they were loaded on to army trucks which took them to Rangoon Military Hospital where they underwent medical inspection. Those who were ill or injured were immediately treated or hospitalised. Eber was one of the luckier ones.

*'Due to the good food, during my two weeks stay at Takuri Camp, I was discharged from the hospital. It was the 27th September.'*

With a clean bill of health and a new kit he then boarded the SS ACMA the next day. There were thousands of ex-POWs aboard. Many, due to rough seas, became seasick. On October 2nd, the SS ACMA steamed into Madras harbour. They were given a royal welcome as ships of all shapes and sizes sounded their sirens in welcome.

Eber and his friends were elated by their warm welcome. Madras harbour, its godowns and other buildings were gaily decked out in buntings and the flags of the United Nations. The ex-POWs were welcomed by official contingents of the British and Indian Red Cross Societies. There was a reception during which they were given more supplies of food and cigarettes. After this, they were escorted to Sadakoo Hospital, where they rested for a few days. Later, Eber left for Bombay where he had arranged to meet his wife, Mabel.

They stayed in Bombay for a few months, then they decided to tour India. He recalls the beauty of many of India's cities, its mountains and resorts. They were in a group of ex-POWs and their wives who visited New Delhi, Naini Tal, Darjeeling and Kashmir. The party then returned to Bombay and were officially informed that they were to return to their homeland. Preparations were made for their journey.

A few days later they embarked on a train which took them from Bombay across the Indian desert. From there, they travelled to Calcutta arriving in the evening. It was as Eber recalls, teeming with crowds of people. They were taken by truck to a camp where they rested for the night. Early the next morning, they were taken to the harbour where they boarded a ship for home. It was a fairly uneventful crossing and they enjoyed life aboard ship. The seas were relatively calm and nobody became seriously seasick.

A few days later, their ship arrived in Singapore harbour. Their welcome was low-key. The island was then under the administration of the British Military government. After Eber had brought his wife home he then went to report to the Singapore Volunteer Corps Headquarters in Beach Road. Then he went home.

The next day Eber reported for work at school. He was back at his old school. Nothing seemed to have changed. He saw, he said, some of the old faces, but then realised that some were missing. Upon enquiry he was sadly told that a male teacher had been taken away by the Japanese to be shot. Nobody seemed to know why. Eber also noticed that a Japanese woman teacher was no longer employed there. She had been repatriated to her homeland.

*'I received, after the war, some letters from my former Japanese pupils. But I did not reply to the letters at all because I still cannot forget the treatment by the Japanese.*

*'In fact if you were to give me free trip to Japan, I would just refuse to accept, because I cannot forget what the Japanese have done to me.'*

# WAR MEMORIALS

'They shall grow not old as we that are left to grow old;
Age shall not weary them nor the years condemn;
At the going down of the sun and in the morning,
We will remember them.'

Laurence Binyon

On Saturday, 15th February 1992, a Fiftieth Anniversary Memorial Service was held at the Kranji War Cemetery in Singapore. It was a service which was dedicated to the memory of the men and women who died during the Second World War 1942-45. A memorial plaque was also unveiled.

The service started at 7.15 am with buglers, drummers, pipers and an honour guard. Wreaths were laid. Members who took part, among them Cleaver Rowell Eber, were the Ex-Services Association of Singapore, the Ex-Prisoners of War Association of Australia, the Eighth Australian Division Association, the Royal British Legion, the Far Eastern Prisoners of War Clubs Association and the Oldham and District Far East Prisoners of War Association.

Similar memorial services were held in other countries. It was an Act of Remembrance to honour those who had given their lives for their countries. Many of the ex-POWS had made the sad pilgrimage from around the world to pay homage to battle comrades of fifty years ago, from India, Australia, Malaysia,

Britain and Singapore. Mr David Knowles, CBE, National Chairman of the Royal British Legion paid tribute to the fallen with excerpts from the *Eulogy of Pericles.* Mr Ken Gray a war veteran and President of the Eight Australian Division Association quoted the poet Lilliard:

'Fear not that you have died for naught;
The torch you threw to us we caught!
And now our hands will hold it high,
Its glorious light will never die.
We'll not break faith with you who lie on many a field.'

The Association Prayer of Thanksgiving was recited by Mr Charles Simon, Past President of the Ex-Services' Association of Singapore. Prayers of Remembrance were said by the leaders of the Inter-Religious Organisation of Singapore. The Reverend Harry Hopkins, RD, RNR, a Committee Member of the Ex-Services' Association of Singapore gave the Blessing. It was a very moving sight to see wives, husbands, sons, daughters and friends walk slowly along the pathways between the graves and lay their own bouquets or wreaths for their beloved dead, say a silent prayer or shed a tear and then move slowly on. The war memorial cemetery is in the north of the island and was once a scene of bitter fighting during World War II.

Now, as the sun began to peep from behind the clouds, Kranji looked like a peaceful haven for those men and women of so many nations who gave their lives for an ideal.

As Mr Ken Gray, President of the Eighth Australian Division Association in his Prologue said:

*'On this Special Day, with heavy hearts and tearful eyes, let us think of them as they were, and remember that their sacrifice is the very fuel that keeps the lights of freedom and liberty ablaze.'*

The land for the Allied POWs war dead in Siam was

*11th October, 1989. Her Majesty Queen Elizabeth II visits Kranji War Memorial and talks to C. R. Eber, second from right.*

purchased in 1946. It is in Ban Don Ruk in the northern part of Kanchanaburi. It honours the Allied POWs who died while building the bridge over the River Kwai. Here lie 6,982 Allied soldiers from Australia, New Zealand and Britain.

Initially, the graves were marked by neat, white wooden crosses. But as these deteriorated in the tropical weather, they were replaced by golden crosses faced onto stone. The cemetery is filled with shady trees and fragrant flower beds. Different countries have different days on which they hold memorial services for their war dead.

New Zealand holds its memorial service on April 25, while the Dutch honour their dead on May 5th; the British have a memorial service usually attended by members of the Royal Family on November 11 each year. Wreaths of red poppies, the sign of remembrance, are laid on the Cenotaph in London's Whitehall. Her Majesty Queen Elizabeth II usually places the official wreath followed by other dignitaries. It always is a solemn and moving annual ceremony watched by thousands.

# THE SANCTITY OF LIFE

Cleaver Rowell Eber now aged 84 years lives with his second wife, Phyllis, in a flat in Marine Parade, on Singapore's East Coast. I spoke to him a few days ago to ask him about his feelings in view of his World War II experiences as a POW about the sanctity of life. He indicated that he felt very strongly about it and that the words of the Roman Catholic Archbishop of Singapore, the Rt. Reverend Gregory Yong's recent Pastoral Letter, read in all Roman Catholic Churches in October 1995, best summed up his feelings.

Eber has a profound respect for his Grace and he insisted that I publish his pastoral Letter in full in 'his book'.

The Pastoral Letter is entitled: 'Respect for Human Life.'

All life comes from God but only man is created in the image and likeness of God (Genesis 1:26-28 and 2:18-25). It is from God that human life derives its sanctity and dignity. This dignity is inviolable and its value does not depend upon certain conditions or perfection of that life. The Church has spoken out with increasing frequency in defence of the sacredness and inviolability of human life and this is once again stressed most recently by Pope John Paul II when he says:

If such great care must be taken to respect every life, even that of criminals and unjust aggressors, the commandment,

"You shall not kill" has absolute value when it refers to an innocent person. And all the more so in the case of the weak and defenceless human beings . . . In effect, the absolute inviolability of innocent human life is a moral truth, clearly taught by Sacred Scriptures, constantly upheld in the Church's tradition and consistently proposed by her Magisterium.

(Evangelium Vitae, no. 57, para 1 and 2)

The Church is totally opposed to any action committed against life (Gaudium et Spes no 27). The Congregation for the Doctrine of the Faith in its Declaration on Euthanasia and again quoted by Pope John Paul II in the same encyclical above teaches that:

Nothing and no one can in any way permit the killing of an innocent human being, whether a foetus or embryo, an infant or an adult, an old person or one suffering from an incurable disease, or a person who is dying. Furthermore, no one is permitted to ask for this act of killing either for himself or herself, or for another person entrusted to his or her care, nor can he or she consent to it explicitly or implicitly. Nor can any authority legitimately recommend or permit such an action. (ibid no. 57 para 5)

But the Church does recognise a person's self-determination in making medical decisions including refusal of life-sustaining treatment. The Advance Medical Directive is the extension of this right of the individual to seek or not to seek medical treatment but in this context, it refers to the terminally ill with very little hope of recovery.

The Catechism of the Catholic Church in number 2278 says:

'Discontinuing medical procedures that are burdensome, dangerous, extraordinary or disproportionate to the expected outcome can be legitimate. It is the refusal of over-zealous treatment. Here one does not will to cause death; one's inability to impede it is merely accepted.'

The decision should be made by the patient if he is competent and able, or if not, by those legally entitled to act for the patient, whose reasonable will and legitimate interests must always be respected.'

In Christian understanding, human life is the most fundamental of goods but concrete bodily existence is the highest of values. We need not cling on to life at all cost, neither should we destroy life when it becomes frustrating. We are only called to a responsible stewardship of this life. Holy Father in the above encyclical, no.65 para 2 says:

Euthanasia must be distinguished from the decision to forego so-called aggressive medical treatment, in other words, medical procedures which no longer correspond to the real situation of the patient, either because by now they are disproportionate to any expected results or because they impose an excessive burden on the patient and his family. In such situations, when death is clearly imminent and inevitable, one can in conscience refuse forms of treatment that would only secure a precarious and burdensome prolongation of life, so long as the normal care due to the sick person in similar cases is not interrupted. Certainly there is a moral obligation to care for oneself and to allow oneself to be cared for, but this duty must take account of concrete circumstances. It needs to be determined whether the means of treatment available are objectively proportionate to the prospect of improvement. To forego extraordinary or disproportionate means is not the equivalent of suicide or euthanasia, it rather expresses acceptance of the human condition in the face of death.

While not opposing the concept of the living will or as it is now called, the Advance Medical Directive, the Church is aware of its strong connection to euthanasia. This progression has been seen in many countries and constitutes a real danger because people can become so desensitized that the logical progression of not wanting treatment to wanting to die is obscured. The necessity and usefulness of the Advance Medical Directive is questionable as such legislation in other countries has achieved very little. On the contrary, it raises enormous complexities, both medically and legally. The traditional method of consultation between doctors and family members (or the patient whenever possible) is adequate. In normal medical practice treatment may be withdrawn by a doctor when in his medical judgement, it is deemed useless. He is not mandated by law to render useless treatment nor does standard medical care require useless treatment. Common law already provides this breadth and it suffices.

A few days after my meeting with Cleaver Rowell Eber he wrote to me. He had a few more comments to make and he had written it in his own neat writing on small sheets of paper. This is what he said:

'I read in the *Straits Times* issue dated 5th October 1991 that a certain Japanese national named Koichiro Ishikawa tried to gain sympathy for Japan by stating that the West was responsible for the carnage of World War II and so the West must take its share for the blame for the war. He further stated that it was the West that plundered and colonised countries like India and the major parts of Africa and so Japan should be given a free hand to plunder and occupy countries too'.

Eber felt that the misdeeds of the colonial west do not give any country the right to invade and terrorise its weaker neighbours. He said that Mr Ishikawa also defended Iraq's invasion of Kuwait when he said that Iraq was trapped into fighting the Gulf War. Eber believes his statements are entirely false for it was Iraq that invaded Kuwait.

'I fear for the future of Asia, especially when Japan is upgrading its military influence. I wonder how many other Japanese share his views. Mr Ishikawa even had the audacity to say that the attack on Pearl Harbour (World War II) was a daring military victory in Japanese history. I dare to say that the attack on Pearl Harbour showed a cowardly mentality of the Japanese High Command,' contends Eber.

He believes that the unscrupulous, unwarranted atrocities of the Japanese forces in China and Manchuria were fully compensated when the Atomic bomb exploded over the two cities of Hiroshima and Nagasaki, killing 100,000 civilians. He also thought that the writer (Ishikawa) had forgotten the 'Rape of Nanking' (China) when more than 300,000 Chinese civilians were slaughtered by the Japanese.

Eber continues: 'I believe that every year the Japanese observe a festival called "bo nien kai" to help them forget the events of the past years. Strangely, the Japanese choose to remember the injustices they had suffered in the last war, but not the cruelties they had inflicted on others, especially the Chinese and the Koreans.'

Eber believes that no one should condone imperialism in any form, especially a country which had caused the deaths of millions of people in Asia during the war. Japan, he contends, has altered its history books and distorted facts and he strongly believes that it 'has done a grave wrong to its future generations.'

With reference to the war-torn cities of Hiroshima and Nagasaki Eber says:

'Although Japan had every right to mourn the thousands of civilians killed in Hiroshima and Nagasaki, she must also show remorse for the millions of lives taken by her occupation forces in the Pacific during the war.' If it had not been for the atomic bombs that forced the Japanese to surrender on August 15th 1945, Eber dreads to think of the outcome of the last

106

world war. Indeed he believes that the death toll would have been much higher. Entire populations would have been decimated.

He says that the spectre of military renewal in Japan has been confronted by loud protests from many quarters, not only from within Japan but from all parts of the world. He believes that the Japanese people must accept the painful truth that military aggressors will definitely suffer in the end.

He feels strongly that if Japan is truly apologetic about the war, it should admit its mistakes and apologise directly to all concerned.

'I would like to know if the Japanese Consul general in Singapore, had summoned Mr. Ishikawa to his office with regard to his statement that the west must take the blame for World War II and to stop him giving his comments to the press.'